A working-class fighter wins release from prison

"I can't live quietly in a world where over thirty Black churches are burned to the ground in eighteen months; where U.S. troops roam the globe at will to make things safe for big-business interests; a world that creates the kind of hell I just came from." That's what Mark Curtis told supporters who greeted him as he walked out the gate of the Iowa State Penitentiary on June 18, 1996.

Curtis knew he was back among fellow working-class fighters. Among those who met him at the prison gates was David Ochoa, a packinghouse worker in Perry, Iowa, originally from Guatemala. Also there were Frankie Travis, one of the union "Road Warriors" who traveled the country to win solidarity after he and his co-workers were locked out by the A.E. Staley Company in Decatur, Illinois; Joel Britton from the Socialist Workers Party National Committee; James Harris, the SWP candidate for president of the United States; Hazel Zimmerman, a longtime leader of the Mark Curtis Defense Committee; and Tom Alter, a leader of the Young Socialists from Bloomington, Indiana.

This was a fitting welcome for a socialist and unionist

KRISTIN MERIAM

Supporters meeting Curtis when he walked out of prison on June 18, 1996. Left: David Ochoa, packinghouse worker from Perry, Iowa. Right: Tom Alter (left), leader of the Young Socialists from Bloomington, Indiana, and Joel Britton (middle), member of the National Committee of the Socialist Workers Party.

who had spent seven and a half years behind bars on frame-up charges before winning release on parole. It marked the culmination of an eight-year nonpartisan defense campaign that had involved thousands of people around the world. A caravan of supporters drove with Curtis, first to Peoria, Illinois, for a lunch celebration, and then on to Chicago, where he was looking forward to rejoining the class struggle.

Mark Curtis's story gives insight into a chapter of working-class struggle in the United States. His victory says a lot about the continued resistance to government and employer assaults on working people and the oppressed, both in the United States and around the world.

Curtis's fight for justice began in March 1988, when the twenty-nine-year-old meatpacker was arrested by the Des Moines police, beaten, and falsely charged with attempting to rape a Black teenager. At the time he was involved in a fight to defend seventeen co-workers at the Swift packinghouse who had just been arrested in an immigration raid. He was also active in fights against police racism, to oppose government spying, and in support of labor struggles, especially in the Midwest.

Curtis's fight against the frame-up won broad international support. But in September 1988 he was convicted in an unfair trial and sentenced to twenty-five years in prison. Over the years thousands of people around the world wrote to the Iowa Board of Parole and other Iowa officials demanding his release. He was denied parole several times. But as time passed more and more people began to ask, "Why is Mark Curtis still in prison?" Almost exactly seven years from the date of his sentencing, on November 21, 1995, the parole board granted Curtis's request to be released to Illinois.

State stalls release from prison

Getting from that day to the moment he walked out of prison is a story in itself. Curtis, like many other workers who do time behind bars, learned that the state has many ways of stalling. And any "incident" that may occur in prison can be used to revoke the parole order. This is part of the degrading and dehumanizing treatment to which inmates are regularly subjected in this country. When the prisoner is a victim of a political frame-up, as in Curtis's case, the stakes are that much higher.

Curtis had asked to be paroled to Chicago because his wife, Kate Kaku, lives there and he had offers of employment in the city. Chicago is a place where there are many opportunities to work in industry and where Curtis could belong to a branch of the Socialist Workers Party, of which he has been a member since 1979.

After Iowa officials agreed to the parole, Curtis still had to be accepted by Illinois parole officials. On February 16, 1996, Illinois officials told Curtis's lawyer they were denying the parole request on the grounds that he did not have any "family" in the state. They said his ten-year relationship with Kaku did not count because they were not formally married.

At the same time Curtis faced a new form of harassment in prison. Although the framed-up unionist often contributed to the socialist weekly the *Militant*, including a regular column, "From Behind Prison Walls," three articles that he mailed for publication between mid-December and mid-February never arrived. Prison officials did not respond to inquiries about them.

"There can be no justification for these repeated violations of freedom of speech and freedom of the press guaranteed in the U.S. Constitution," *Militant* editor Steve Clark wrote to the warden at the Iowa State Penitentiary, demanding the release of Curtis's articles. Dozens of others also wrote protesting the censorship. Finally prison officials, while not admitting censorship, backed down and a new column for the *Militant*, describing discussions about the Cuban revolution among prisoners in Fort Madison, arrived in early March.

Curtis and Kaku formalized their marriage and he resubmitted the application for parole to Illinois. Meanwhile, defense committee supporters wrote to Curtis in prison, expressing determination to continue the fight and reverse the delay in his parole. They also went on a campaign to win new supporters to the fight, using the earlier edition of this pamphlet, *Why Is Mark Curtis Still in Prison?*

NAOMI CRAINE

Curtis selling literature at Socialist Workers campaign table in Chicago in August 1996.

There were other attacks during this period as well. In December, there was an attempted arson at the Pathfinder bookstore in Des Moines. The bookstore housed the international offices of the Mark Curtis Defense Committee from its formation in 1988 until it moved to Chicago in February 1996, in anticipation of Curtis's parole there. The arsonist lit a fire that did considerable smoke damage hours after a highly publicized celebration of Curtis's parole victory, and two days after a Militant Labor Forum at the bookstore opposing the deployment of U.S. troops to Yugoslavia. A wide range of unionists, farmers, and other supporters of democratic rights condemned the bookstore attack and called on city authorities to carry out a serious investigation and prosecute those responsible.

In March, Iowa officials sent the paperwork for Curtis's parole to Illinois for the second time. The authorities there continued to stall and again turned down the application, saying they had no evidence that Curtis had a support network in Illinois. In one week, Curtis's supporters gathered more than forty letters demonstrating the backing he did have in the state, including two offering employment. Illinois parole officials finally relented, and on June 18, 1996, Curtis won his freedom.

Back in the class struggle

Within a month he was back working in an industrial plant. At a "Welcome back to the class struggle" celebration in Chicago in August, Curtis described his job. "I've been there now for a about a month, in a union-organized plant that plastic-coats steel parts, working on the spray line and getting calluses back on my hands. The plant is overwhelmingly Mexican, with a handful of Black workers, and one white guy—me. My presence there was something of a surprise to many who thought I would be working as their supervisor in the office. But after they see that I do the same jobs and under the same conditions of heat, dirt, and sweat, and speak with them in Spanish, they like it.

"One of the first political discussions I've had at work is over the recent arrest of some forty immigrant workers at an electronics plant in Elk Grove. Those arrested by *la migra* included two pregnant women who weren't even given the opportunity to see their families before they were taken away," he said.

Curtis described other experiences he'd been having on the job and in political work in the city, where he immediately got involved in work in defense of immigrant rights and in support of the Cuban revolution. He described selling socialist papers and books at rail yards and earlier

JOEL BRITTON

August 1996 "Welcome back to the class struggle" rally in Chicago. (From left to right) Naomi Craine; Mark Curtis; Tom Alter; David Marshall, SWP leader from Peoria, Illinois; Linda Jenness, former secretary of Defense Committee.

that day on a Socialist Workers campaign table.

"I'm doing all of these things in spite of certain restrictions that go along with being on parole," Curtis said. These conditions include not traveling outside Cook County, Illinois, without permission; not returning to Polk County, Iowa, where Des Moines is; and having to register with the cops as having been convicted as a "sex offender." This last stipulation comes under antidemocratic regulations passed in many states and signed into federal law in May 1996 by President William Clinton.

"But having said that, it's important to note things have gone as well as could have been hoped for," Curtis said.

"I went into prison a communist and I came out one too, a stronger one in fact, due to collaboration with the Socialist Workers Party, my studies of books published by Pathfinder Press, reading the *Militant* regularly, and holding discussion groups with other prisoners interested in these ideas," he said. Curtis was elected to the SWP National Committee in 1994, while he was in prison, and has served actively on that body since then.

At the meeting Linda Jenness, who until then had served as secretary of the Mark Curtis Defense Committee, announced that the committee "is no more, because we don't need one. Mark is a free man."

John Studer, the long-time coordinator of the defense committee, told the seventy people gathered for the event that the files of the committee were being sent to the State Historical Society in Madison, Wisconsin. This institution will preserve the collection, making the record and lessons of the eight-year fight available for activists and political researchers.

The Political Rights Defense Fund, Inc. (PRDF), of which Studer is the executive director, will take responsibility for any further legal expenses Curtis faces while on parole, he explained. PRDF is a nonpartisan organization founded in 1973 to gather backing and funds for the landmark lawsuit filed by the SWP and Young Socialist Alliance challenging the decades-long campaign of the FBI and other government agencies to spy on, harass, and disrupt the two socialist groups. PRDF has also supported other defense efforts, the most prominent being that of Héctor Marroquín, a young socialist from Mexico who the U.S. government tried to deport in the 1980s. The records of these two fights and many other defense cases are also preserved at the Madison archives.

Young Socialists leader Tom Alter and Naomi Craine, speaking on behalf of the SWP National Committee, pointed to many of these other fights in their talks at the

NAOMI CRAINE

Turning the files of the Mark Curtis Defense Committee over to the State Historical Society of Wisconsin in October 1996. (From left to right) Richard Pifer, head of collections development for the historical society's archives division; John Studer, former defense committee coordinator; Mark Curtis.

celebration. Alter spoke about how an earlier generation of young revolutionists were steeled by the fight to defend three members of the Young Socialist Alliance (YSA) framed up on sedition charges in 1963 in Bloomington, Indiana, for attending a speech on the fight for Black rights by YSA leader Leroy McRae. Craine pointed to a number of other cases: the jailing of eighteen leaders of the SWP and Teamsters union in Minneapolis during World War II under the Smith Act for the "crime" of speaking out against U.S. imperialism's entry into the war; the successful eight-year fight of James Kutcher to win back his government job from the witch-hunters in the 1950s; the case of Joe Johnson, a U.S.-born socialist who Washington tried to deport in the 1960s; and the fight to defend Héctor Marroquín. The materials published on all of these cases do much more than appeal for a broad defense of democratic rights. Each is a lesson in the history of working-class struggle.

The same is true of this pamphlet, which first appeared as a series in the *Militant* in 1993. It was originally published in March 1995 under the title *Why Is Mark Curtis Still in Prison?* Supporters of the defense fight used it to reach out broadly to all those who would ask that question. It also describes Curtis's party, the kind of fighters who belong to it, and the struggles he was and is part of. The story that follows has sparked the interest of workers and young rebels around the world, from the United States to South Africa, from New Zealand to Cuba.

2

INS raid and the Swift 17

On March 4, 1988, several Mexican-born workers at the Swift Independent Packing Company in Des Moines, Iowa, walked off the line, stopping production. They demanded to be allowed to attend a meeting to protest the arrest of seventeen co-workers at the meatpacking plant by the immigration cops three days earlier.

A few hours later a young Swift worker, Mark Curtis, was arrested by the Des Moines police and taken to the city jail. In a small room police officers ordered him to undress, placed a tape recorder on a desk, and began to interrogate him. Curtis said he wanted a lawyer, but the police continued their questions. When he refused to answer without legal counsel, the cops beat him, saying he was a "Mexican lover, just like you love those coloreds." Another cop told him, "I'll bet you've got AIDS."

Curtis was knocked unconscious and suffered a blowout fracture to his eye socket. Fifteen stitches were needed to close the gash on his face. When the cops took him to the hospital to be sewn up, they told hospital workers Curtis was a rapist who had AIDS. He woke up shackled to a hospital bed. Afterward he was taken back to jail and thrown in a cell for the night—naked, bleeding, and without a towel, blanket, bedding, or toilet facilities. The twenty-nine-year-old union activist and socialist was charged with attempting to rape a Black teenager and with two counts of assaulting the police who beat him bloody. So began the frame-up of Mark Curtis.

Curtis did not get a fair trial. He was denied the right to present key evidence to the jury. In September 1988 he was convicted on false charges of third-degree sexual abuse and first-degree burglary. Two months later he was sentenced to twenty-five years in prison.

* * *

To understand what happened to Mark Curtis and why working people had a stake in joining the effort to win his release, it is important to go back to the raid the Immigration and Naturalization Service (INS) conducted at the Swift packinghouse. On March 1, three days before Curtis's arrest, federal marshals and local police swooped down on the factory in a well-organized raid and arrested seventeen immigrant workers—sixteen from Mexico and one from El Salvador. It turned out the raid had actually been planned months in advance with Swift's direct involvement.

INS agents had gone into the company's personnel office, culled through the records of every single worker, and come up with a list of names of the people they were going to arrest. They put the seventeen names in a sealed indictment. Like Curtis, many of the people arrested March 1 were working on the kill floor. The Swift 17, as they became known, were brought up on a variety of felony charges for having falsified documents, such as Social Security numbers and employment eligibility forms, in order to get jobs.

STU SINGER

Héctor Marroquín, Kate Kaku, and Curtis explaining frame-up at Swift packinghouse in Des Moines, spring 1988. Marroquín, a Mexican-born socialist, won an eleven-year fight against U.S. government attempts to deport him.

The raid took place as the INS was trying to convince more undocumented immigrants to apply for amnesty under the 1986 Immigration Reform and Control Act. The amnesty made it possible for a small layer of those without documents to gain legal status. The Swift raid was seen by many as a federally organized probe to legitimize the illegal use of confidential information disclosed on amnesty applications to victimize the undocumented. At least seven of the workers the INS picked up at Swift had already submitted their amnesty applications. This fact helped fuel outrage among working people in Des Moines and beyond, especially in the Latino community.

Immediately following the arrests, family members and friends of the Swift workers gathered outside the Polk County Jail in downtown Des Moines, demanding their release. These supporters were not even allowed to speak to the prisoners.

One of the Swift 17, Martín Castillo, pointed to the hypocrisy of the INS. "I'm confused about everything because they say we falsified our Social Security cards," he told the *Wall Street Journal*. "I don't deny that, but why did they encourage us to apply [for amnesty] and say they wouldn't prosecute us for what we did in our past?" An INS deputy district director answered Castillo's question by telling the *Journal,* "Just because you are an applicant or have been given amnesty, it doesn't mean we are going to forgive your past sins."

3

March 4, 1988

The arrests at Swift sparked a raging discussion among workers at the plant. Some had applauded when the immigration cops came in and arrested the seventeen, because they bought into the bosses' propaganda that immigrant workers "take American jobs." Such prejudices help management at companies like Swift to keep wages low and conditions poor, not just for immigrants but for the entire workforce. The employers and supervisors refer to Mexican workers as *mojados*—"wetbacks" in Spanish—and Asian women as prostitutes. They try to keep people divided and encourage racism in the workforce.

On the job Curtis had helped to unify workers at Swift. He spoke Spanish, which he learned as a teenager. When the immigration police arrested seventeen of his co-workers, Curtis jumped into the discussions in the plant, arguing that the union should join in the fight to defend them. He had previously helped some of the seventeen fill out their amnesty applications.

As anger mounted against the arrests, activists in the Des Moines Latino community called a meeting for 2:00

P.M. on Friday, March 4. The forum, held at the United Mexican-American Community Center near the Swift plant, was set up to provide an opportunity for Swift workers and others to protest the raid and get some answers about the arrests and the amnesty program. Swift management had originally agreed to allow any worker who wanted to go to this meeting to do so. But when 2:00 P.M. came around, the company refused to allow the workers to leave, saying they had to keep the line in operation until five hundred cattle had been killed and cut.

Workers walk off the line
Outraged by this action, a number of workers walked off the line to attend the meeting, shutting down the line. It was the first such job action there anyone could remember. The company was forced to back down. They agreed to make it possible for the workers to attend a later meeting and asked the organizers to hold such a meeting at 5:00 P.M. Curtis attended that meeting along with many other workers at Swift.

More than one hundred family members, supporters of the Swift workers, and community activists came to the first meeting. INS district director James Cole, accompanied by Des Moines cops and Swift officials, spoke at that meeting and was denounced by family members and friends of the arrested workers. Alfredo Alvarez, then chairperson of the Des Moines Human Rights Commission, and others proposed organizing a protest march, which was called for March 12.

About two dozen workers from Swift attended the second meeting, and some participants in the first one stayed over to continue the discussion. "It was mostly guys from the kill floor. Company representatives were there as well," Curtis said later. "Speaking in Spanish, I said, 'We need to get the union involved. It's not just an issue for the workers arrested, it's an attack on everybody in the plant.' I volunteered to begin to reach out to the rest of the workers at Swift.

"After the meeting I went with my co-workers to a nearby bar, Los Compadres, to have more discussion," Curtis said. "There were some other workers there too, and they were inspired by the militancy of the Mexican workers in the walkout that day. 'That's the way we should do it every time the foremen mess with us,' one said."

The arrest

Curtis left the bar around 8:30 P.M. that evening and went home. He was expecting two friends from out of town to arrive any minute. One of them, Kevin Magee, was sched-

STU SINGER

March 12, 1988, demonstration in Des Moines in defense of seventeen workers arrested at Swift.

uled to speak the next night on a recent trip to Nicaragua at a Militant Labor Forum Curtis was organizing.

Curtis had to go to the grocery store to buy food for a dinner before the forum, so he called a couple of friends who lived nearby, Ellen Whitt and Jackie Floyd, to let them know where he would be and to ask them to look out for his guests. At the trial Floyd, who worked midnight shift at the Firestone Tire and Rubber plant in Des Moines, testified that she received Curtis's call at 8:45 that evening. She knew the exact time because he had awakened her and she had looked at the clock to see if she had to get up for work.

About five blocks from his house, Curtis stopped at a red light. A young Black woman approached his car. She looked very upset and begged him to give her a ride to her house. She said a man at the nearby TNT bar was after her. Curtis knew that a woman had been killed in that bar recently. He was particularly concerned about violence against women because one of his sisters had been raped.

Curtis let the woman get into his car and offered to call the police. She said she didn't want him to do that and asked for a ride home. She directed him to a house and asked him to come up on the porch with her because she was afraid the man might be inside. The woman went into the house, while Curtis waited on the porch. He never saw her again. A minute or so later the porch door behind him flew open. Curtis thought at first it was the man the woman was scared of. But it was the cops.

One of the police officers, Joseph Gonzalez, grabbed Curtis by the arm and shouted "I got him." Curtis assumed the woman had called them and they mistakenly thought he was the man who was after her. Gonzalez walked Curtis through the living room into the back bedroom. He handcuffed Curtis's hands behind his back.

The cop then pushed Curtis onto the bed, undid his pants,

and pulled them down. "Let's see what we got here," said Gonzalez. The frame-up of Mark Curtis began right there. Gonzalez took Curtis's wallet and keys and placed him under arrest. Curtis was taken out of the house without even being allowed to fasten his pants.

The next day the *Des Moines Register* printed an article headlined "Boy, 11, calls police, prevents rape of sister." The article stated that Curtis had been arrested while attempting to rape a fifteen-year-old high school student and that a call to the police from her brother had saved the day.

4

A political frame-up

When the Des Moines cops arrested Mark Curtis on March 4, 1988, one of the first things they did was to take his car keys. Among the items they would have noticed in his car, which was parked in front of the house, were several copies of a leaflet advertising an upcoming meeting titled "Stop Government Attacks on Political Rights!"

The flyer listed a variety of examples of democratic rights abuses, including FBI spying against political organizations, the case of the Swift 17, and a recent incident of racist police activity in nearby Clive, Iowa. The police discovery of this leaflet, and the racist remarks of the cops who bloodied Curtis at the station house later that night, made clear what his real crime was: fighting for the rights of working people, including those who speak a different language, come from a different country, or have a different skin color from the wealthy families who rule Des Moines and the rest of the United States.

The struggles for justice detailed on the leaflet in Curtis's car sum up the kind of political activities in which he was deeply involved. There is no mystery why the Des

Moines police and prosecutors indicted the young unionist on rape and burglary charges and railroaded him to prison.

The political frame-up was under way.

Flyer for March 27, 1988, meeting. On finding this leaflet in his car, the cops would have known Curtis was a political activist.

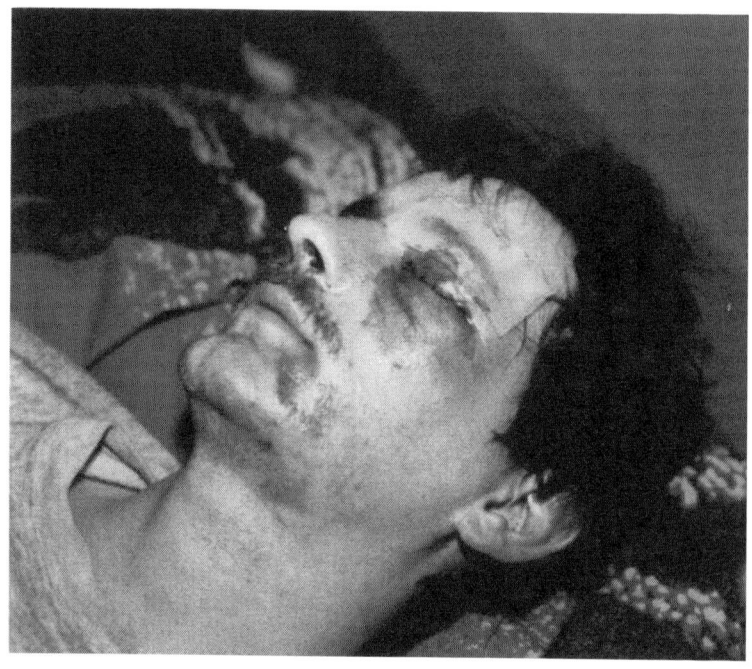

STU SINGER

Curtis after beating by Des Moines cops. Fifteen stitches were needed to close the gash in his face. Picture was taken the day after his arrest.

The leaflet announced a March 27 meeting to "take up many cases of government attacks on political and democratic rights." The meeting was sponsored by the Political Rights Defense Fund (PRDF).

Fight against government spying

"PRDF," the leaflet said, "is organizing the 15 year long fight of the Socialist Workers Party and Young Socialist Alliance suit against government spying and harassment. That suit won a historic decision by Federal Judge Thomas Griesa in August 1986 upholding the right of privacy to advocate political ideas. But Attorney General [Edwin] Meese is appealing the decision."

Just two weeks after Curtis was arrested, the U.S. government withdrew its appeal, and the March 27 meeting was turned into a victory celebration. Curtis, a member of the SWP and former national secretary of the YSA, spoke at that event. He explained that the ruling in the lawsuit was an important weapon in the fight against the cops' attempt to frame him.

The case represented a major victory for the right to carry out political activity in the United States. The SWP and YSA had filed their lawsuit against the FBI and other government police agencies in 1973, charging that the government had illegally spied on and disrupted the organizations. They asked for a court injunction to end these activities, which had been going on at least since 1941.

In 1986 Judge Griesa, who had been appointed by Republican president Richard Nixon, ruled that decades of spying had not revealed any evidence of illegal activity on the part of the SWP and YSA. Instead, he wrote, FBI informers collected "thousands of reports recording peaceful, lawful activity by the SWP and YSA." The snoops also carried out FBI orders to "suppress recruiting activities," to "frustrate the growth of the organizations," and "to attempt to disrupt them."

In his decision, Griesa detailed some of the fifty-seven disruption operations conducted by the FBI, including poison-pen letters, covert attempts to get SWP members fired from their jobs, and efforts to disrupt collaboration between the SWP and Black rights and anti–Vietnam War groups. The decision also documented 20,000 days of wiretaps between 1943 and 1963, as well as 208 FBI burglaries of both SWP offices and homes of its members.

In 1987 the two socialist groups won a further injunction barring the government from using the information contained in the 10 million pages of illegal files uncovered through the lawsuit. The court awarded the SWP and YSA $264,000 in damages as well. The FBI, CIA, INS, and several other government spy agencies had filed affidavits arguing against the injunction. They claimed that any restrictions on use of the illegally obtained files would cripple their functioning and endanger "national security." With the Iran-contra scandal unfolding in 1988, Washington decided not to pursue an appeal of the injunction, which would have put a further spotlight on the government's illegal activities at home.

Antiwar activists targeted

Shortly after the SWP and YSA won the 1987 injunction, another FBI spy operation was exposed. This one targeted the Committee in Solidarity with the People of El Salvador (CISPES) and other opponents of U.S. government policy in Central America.

The Center for Constitutional Rights and CISPES forced the government to admit that, between 1981 and at least 1985, the FBI had collected 3,700 pages of files on hundreds of antiwar activists and other individuals simply on the basis of their political beliefs and activities.

At a news conference in Des Moines following his arrest, Curtis made public the files the FBI had kept on him as part of the spying operation against CISPES. Curtis had participated in antiwar activities in Birmingham, Alabama, from 1981 to 1985. In one document, he was listed as one of three individuals "acting in the leadership roles in the Birmingham area" chapter of the organization. Another FBI document described the group's activities. The CISPES chapter, it noted, "had several peaceful protests in Birmingham area. Group protests U.S. involvement in Central America and Caribbean.... Captioned group advocates 'peace—not just absence of war, but nurturing of human life.'"

Also in the FBI's files was a clipping from the November 10, 1983, *Tuscaloosa News* reporting on an antiwar protest in Tuscaloosa, Alabama. The news item mentions that Curtis spoke at the rally, condemning the recent U.S. invasion of Grenada.

The existence of FBI files on Mark Curtis and on the SWP, YSA, and CISPES was one of the important pieces of evidence that Curtis was not permitted to present at his trial.

Struggles in meatpacking industry

Curtis moved to Des Moines in 1986, inspired by another important battle: the resistance of packinghouse workers in the Midwest to attacks by the bosses.

TOM JAAX

Five thousand marched April 12, 1986, to support striking members of United Food And Commercial Workers Local P-9 in Austin, Minnesota. Meatpackers' struggles helped break pattern of concessions to employers by U.S. Labor movement.

The assault against meatpacking workers began in 1982 when Iowa Beef Processors demanded big concessions in wages and work rules at its Dakota City, Nebraska, plant and defeated a strike by the United Food and Commercial Workers (UFCW) union there. Other large packing companies demanded similar cuts and threatened workers with plant closings if they did not give in. By 1985 average wages had been slashed from $10.69 an hour to $8.24 an hour, and twenty-four thousand packinghouse jobs had been eliminated. Injury rates in the industry skyrocketed due to speedup of production.

The pattern of concession contracts promoted by the UFCW officials and voted for by workers held sway for several years. But in the mid-1980s a layer of workers began to resist further attacks on their livelihoods.

In 1985–86 members of UFCW Local P-9 at the Hormel plant in Austin, Minnesota, went on strike. The membership of Local P-9 decided to put up a fight rather than vote for more concessions on the promise that things might get better over the long haul. The strikers began to take control of their local union and reach out for solidarity to unionists and other working people around the country.

The resolute stand of the Hormel workers helped inspire a wave of strikes in the meatpacking industry throughout the Midwest. Many battles faced difficult odds and a number, like the Hormel strike, were eventually defeated. Many workers decided, however, that it was better to fight than just give in to the bosses' demands. These struggles were an important break in the pattern of concessions by the U.S. labor movement.

This fightback is what prompted Curtis and many other members of the Socialist Workers Party to move to the Midwest and set up new branches in Des Moines, Austin, and Omaha, Nebraska. There they joined struggles in the

Curtis (right) at May 1987 rally for striking packinghouse workers, Sioux Falls, South Dakota.

meatpacking industry and fights by farmers to defend their land against foreclosures by the banks.

The packinghouse bosses often responded to fights by workers with intimidation and harassment. Hormel, for instance, fired Bob Langemeier, a union activist at the company's Fremont, Nebraska, plant, for refusing to cross a picket line set up by the P-9 strikers from Austin. Through the fight to regain Langemeier's job, it was revealed that the company had hired a private investigator to spy on his political and union activities. Among other things, the private cop spied on a Militant Labor Forum in Des Moines where Langemeier spoke on the Hormel strike, a meeting Curtis helped organize and took part in. The cop later said he had taped the meeting by perching on a trash dumpster outside and holding a tape recorder to an air vent.

Soon after moving to Des Moines, Curtis was hired at the Swift packing plant. Conditions in the plant were typical of what had been forced on workers in the industry. Wages started as low as $5.40 an hour and topped out at less than $8.00. In 1987 nearly 80 percent of the workers suffered injuries on the job. Because of the excessive line speed, cuts from knives, amputations, and repetitive motion injuries such as carpal tunnel syndrome were common. During the year before Curtis was arrested, Swift had hired three thousand workers into the plant, although only six hundred were employed there at any one time.

Curtis's job at Swift was pulling cattle paunches—a very strenuous task. In December 1987 he injured his back, but the boss refused to let him see a doctor. After a couple of hours, the pain became unbearable and Curtis walked off the line. The company fired him for this, but with the support of his co-workers and his union, he won the job back.

This was an unusual victory at Swift. When Curtis

initially talked to other workers about fighting the firing, most were skeptical. But he explained the importance of the union standing up for its membership in such situations and was able to get the support he needed from the local.

Fight against police racism

The leaflet found in Curtis's car on March 14 raised the need to respond to "racist attacks like the Clive, Iowa, police notice to report 'Black males.'" This referred to another fight Curtis had participated in during the weeks preceding his arrest.

Clive is a small suburb of Des Moines that has very few residents who are Black. In early February 1988 the Clive police department distributed a flyer referring to a recent burglary and describing the suspect as a large Black man. "If you see a black male in your neighborhood at night," the flyer said, "please call the Clive police immediately so that we can try to find out who the individual is."

The flyer outraged many in the area. The National Association for the Advancement of Colored People (NAACP), Iowa Civil Liberties Union, Des Moines Human Rights Commission, many Clive residents, and others sharply condemned this flagrant racism. Some of these forces organized a protest march February 20 outside Clive City Hall. The Clive City Council, feeling the heat, issued a retraction and a letter of apology for the leaflet. The council refused to take disciplinary action against the police chief, however, and the protest went ahead as scheduled.

Curtis was one of about four hundred people who joined the march. At the end of the demonstration, he set up a table on the police department lawn to sell the *Militant* newspaper and socialist books and pamphlets from the Pathfinder bookstore in Des Moines.

Because of his union and political activity since moving to Des Moines in late 1986, Mark Curtis was easy to identify as a staunch fighter for democratic rights and for the interests of Blacks, immigrants, and all working people.

STU SINGER

Curtis with FBI spy files on his activity against U.S. military intervention in Central America.

5

Mark Curtis defense campaign launched

As a union activist and a member of the Socialist Workers Party for many years, Mark Curtis knew it would take a strong political defense campaign to defeat the cops' attempt to railroad him to prison, and he looked to other fighting workers for help. Key to this effort was assembling a public, nonpartisan defense committee to involve all those who wanted to counter what was clearly a political frame-up.

At the March 12, 1988, rally, where some two hundred people gathered to protest the INS raid at Swift, Curtis talked to the media about what had happened to him a little more than a week earlier. He helped pass out a flyer titled "Protest Des Moines police brutality and frame-up." The leaflet asked people to come to a meeting at the Pathfinder bookstore later that day.

More than forty people came, including several workers from the Swift plant, members of the Iowa Citizens Action Network, students from the University of Iowa and Drake University, and Jane Curtis, Mark's mother. They decided to organize a news conference to get out the truth about Curtis's arrest. Curtis also urged people to send telegrams to Des Moines police chief William Moulder demanding the charges against him be dropped and protesting his brutalization by the cops.

The Mark Curtis Defense Committee was formally launched at a March 27 meeting of supporters.

Hazel Zimmerman, for many years the treasurer of the defense committee, was one of those who first met Curtis at the demonstration for the Swift 17. In a 1988 interview

STU SINGER

Curtis being interviewed at March 12, 1988, action to defend Swift 17.

Zimmerman said when she first saw Curtis there, with his face still bruised and cut from the police beating, "I went looking for the facts." After she found them, she added, she went "looking for justice."

Getting Curtis out of jail

When Stu Singer, a friend and political collaborator of Curtis, heard about the arrest on the night of March 4, he immediately called the city jail to find out how much the bail was. But the cops gave Singer the runaround—first denying Curtis was there, then saying they weren't sure, and finally saying they were "processing" someone in the back room and to call back later.

In fact, Curtis was being beaten by the police at that time.

At 8:00 the next morning, a delegation of Curtis's friends, co-workers, and community activists arrived at the jail. After one person signed over their trust fund and five signed over their cars, Curtis's supporters managed to raise the $30,000 bail. Around 2:00 P.M. Curtis was released to go home.

Getting Curtis out of jail in less than twenty-four hours was the first blow to the police frame-up and the beginning of his defense campaign. He got a complete medical checkup, including X rays that showed the cops had shattered his cheekbone when they hit him with a nightstick. Singer was able to photograph Curtis. The picture showed graphically what happened to Curtis that night and was important in his 1992 victory in a civil rights lawsuit against the cops who assaulted him. It helped explain to workers around the world what this case was really about.

Looking broadly for support

Curtis and his supporters in the Mark Curtis Defense Committee reached out broadly to workers, farmers, students, and other advocates of democratic rights to explain the facts of what had happened. They went to union meetings and to factory gates, including at the Swift plant. They took the case to political actions, such as a March 17 protest in Des Moines against Washington's war moves in Central America. Curtis addressed the Des Moines Human Rights Commission and other bodies. He went on a speaking tour, bringing his fight to unionists and political activists in other parts of the country.

At a March 19 news conference in Des Moines—attended by the media as well as some fifty workers, students, antiwar and antiracist fighters, and women's rights activists—Curtis went over the details of his activities the day he was arrested. He made public the files kept on him by the FBI when he was an antiwar activist in Birmingham, Alabama.

By that time, messages of support were already starting to come into Des Moines. The president of the American Agriculture Movement in Iowa, Carroll Nearmyer, wrote,

SYLVIA GIESBRECHT

Edna Griffin and Robert Berry were among the first to protest frame-up of Curtis. Both are longtime political activists in Des Moines.

"As a citizen of the U.S. and a farmer who's very concerned about the common people of the world being pushed around by the governments of the world, the establishment, and police, we have to stand together and fight back."

One of the speakers at the news conference was Pat Kearns, a student at the University of Iowa in Iowa City. He expressed solidarity with Curtis on behalf of himself and seventeen other students who had just been acquitted on criminal trespass charges stemming from an anti-CIA protest.

The May 4, 1988, *Des Moines Register* reported that "Des Moines police have received more than four hundred letters from across the country demanding that charges be dropped against Mark Curtis, the Swift packing plant employee charged with an attempted sex crime. . . . Many of the letters contain petitions signed by dozens of Curtis supporters. Police say some letters even have foreign postmarks."

6

The government, prosecutors, and their friends

From the outset, the Des Moines cops, prosecutors, and city officials sought to undercut the support Curtis was winning. People identifying themselves as representatives of the Des Moines police department and Polk County sheriff's office called some of the people who had sent messages to the police chief protesting Curtis's arrest and beating, asking if they had really written the letters.

Des Moines mayor John Dorrian joined in defending the cops. Doug Womack, president of United Auto Workers Local 893 in Marshalltown, Iowa, had written the mayor March 28 regarding the Curtis case. "I have no idea if the charges of either party are true or not," Womack said, "but I'm not naive enough to think things of this nature don't happen either!" Dorrian wrote back attempting to rebut the defense campaign. The mayor's letter contained many arguments that would be used by the forces supporting the frame-up.

Throwing aside the presumption of innocence, Dorrian began by assuming that since Curtis had been *charged* with sexual abuse and with assaulting two cops, he must be guilty. The mayor repeated the cops' story that while they were interrogating Curtis he "attacked and injured one of the officers. In the course of the restrainment, Mr. Curtis suffered an injury to his right eyebrow." Actually, it was Curtis's left cheekbone that was smashed, requiring fifteen stitches.

Dorrian was also the first to try to discredit Curtis as a political activist—something that would become a hallmark of the campaign waged by supporters of the prosecution's case. While "Curtis is portraying himself as a major social activist who has had prominent roles in protest marches," Dorrian said, "a spokesperson for the local National Council of Christians and Jews organization disclaims the fact that Mr. Curtis is a prominent leader in the community. In addition, Human Rights Commission members did not know of Mr. Curtis prior to his arrest. Hispanic leaders have been consulted and they recognize inconsistencies in his claim."

Curtis replied to the mayor's letter, saying, "I do not claim to be a prominent leader. I have been an activist for more than ten years in opposition to the war in Central America, against racism, in support of women's rights, in defense of immigrants, and in support of unions and farmers."

Curtis went on to explain the kind of rank-and-file union activist he was: "My co-workers, and Swift management too, know I stand up for better safety and working conditions. I speak Spanish and actively defend the rights of immigrant workers." He and his supporters were to explain this point many more times, in answer to those who later challenged his union credentials by pointing out he was not an official.

Others jump on bandwagon
Other forces, in Des Moines and elsewhere, took the side of the cops and prosecutor's office. Keith Morris, the father

of the young woman who accused Curtis of rape, made repeated threats and attacks against Curtis and the Mark Curtis Defense Committee.

In the most serious attack, on July 15, 1988, Morris smashed the storefront windows of the Pathfinder bookstore in Des Moines, where the defense committee rents its office. Curtis was in the bookstore at the time but was able to leave through a different door. Just prior to the attack, Morris had told two cops he was going to "kick ass," but the police did nothing to stop him. At a court hearing three days earlier, Morris had also made threats against Curtis that went unchallenged by the judge.

The authorities refused to press charges against Morris, and the owner of the bookstore had to go to small-claims court, winning a judgment that ordered Morris to pay the $2,000 in damage done to the store.

The prosecution also found support in the Workers League. This outfit, which claims to be socialist, has earned the distrust and hatred of many workers through its disruptive actions in the course of working-class struggles. It specializes in attacking unions on strike, from the United Mine Workers of America to the United Paperworkers International Union and numerous others. The *Bulletin*, the newspaper of the Workers League (later changed to the *International Workers Bulletin*), regularly ran articles attacking Curtis and his defense campaign. During the months leading up to the trial, members of the outfit distributed a statement, titled "The Strange Case of Mark Curtis," promoting the prosecution's arguments.

Some forces, claiming to speak for the rights of women and Blacks in Des Moines, also campaigned to say Curtis was guilty and should be jailed, emphasizing that the fifteen-year-old woman he was accused of attacking is Black.

Activists associated with Polk County Victim Services, an agency that provides counseling to rape victims and others, actively worked to convince people not to support Curtis, accepting the cops' account of what happened as a proven fact. Opponents of the defense effort cited Victim Services director Marti Anderson and others as saying that this "is a good rape case" and "Curtis is guilty."

Members of the Des Moines chapter of the National Black United Front also joined in the prosecution effort to convict Curtis.

7

Presumption of innocence denied

On the eve of Curtis's trial, the breadth of solidarity with his international defense effort was reflected at a September 4, 1988, rally at the Des Moines Civic Center. More than four hundred people turned out to hear a wide array of fighters discuss Curtis's case and how it related to their own experiences in struggles.

Among those speaking at that meeting was veteran civil rights and political activist Edna Griffin, who was then seventy-eight years old. She told the crowd that when she read in the papers that the authorities were going after a white man accused of raping a young Black woman she had wondered, "What's this new arrangement? When has there been such concern about sexual abuse, never mind rape, of our young Black women?"

Griffin answered her own question shortly afterward when, as she told *Militant* reporter Margaret Jayko, "I figured out that he is Spanish-speaking and is a great danger because he can communicate with Spanish-speaking workers." Griffin is right—to the powers-that-be in the state of Iowa, Mark Curtis is indeed a dangerous man.

ERIC SIMPSON

ERIC SIMPSON

Speakers at defense rally in Des Moines, September 4, 1988. Top: (speaking) Jack Barnes, Socialist Workers Party national secretary; (from left to right) Mark Curtis; defense committee activists Ellen Whitt and Nan Bailey; and Hazel Zimmerman, treasurer of Defense Committee. Bottom left: Carroll Nearmyer, American Agriculture Movement. Bottom right: Susan Mnumzana, African National Congress.

The international speakers panel also included Susan Mnumzana, at the time secretary for women's affairs at the United Nations observer mission of the African National

Congress of South Africa; novelist and poet Piri Thomas; and Jack Barnes, national secretary of the Socialist Workers Party.

"Mark Curtis will not get a fair trial," Barnes told the meeting. "The courtroom is not where innocence and guilt will be decided and it is not where justice will be found."

"No one in the world is obligated to prove Mark Curtis's innocence," Barnes said, pointing to the key political considerations that Curtis's backers needed to keep in mind when the trial opened September 7. "The presumption of innocence has taken hundreds of years for working people to win. It is not a legal fiction. It is not something that you have the right to pick or choose, depending on what you like, what you identify with, the individual involved.

"This is very recent in human history," Barnes said. "We shouldn't take it for granted, because the Des Moines police department, the Polk County prosecutor, the Federal Bureau of Investigation, the liberal newspapers, all are trying to take it away. Not only from Mark, but from everyone."

From the point of view of the U.S. capitalist rulers, Barnes continued, working people *are* guilty. That's the presumption. Workers, farmers, and all supporters of democratic rights, on the other hand, cherish the right to presumption of innocence. This is a right that the toilers have fought to wrest from the ruling classes over hundreds of years.

The presumption of innocence, said Barnes, "is one of the most important milestones on the march to human solidarity and to the ability of the great majority of the world to act as fully human beings. No one, I repeat, is obligated to prove Mark Curtis's innocence."

For serfs under feudalism, for Blacks under slavery, and for women during most of the history of class-divided society, Barnes noted, there was no such thing as the presumption of innocence. There was, simply, the lord's, slavemaster's, or husband's property.

"It's not that you are innocent until proven guilty. You are innocent. *Innocent*," Barnes said. "This is a country where everything is the opposite. It's the presumption of guilt that dominates in the 'democratic' United States. Saturday night is open season on any young Black man in the United States, on every young Puerto Rican. It's open season on women much of the time. It's not the presumption of innocence but the horror of guilt."

The rulers' goals in this case are large ones, Barnes explained. "They want cities like Des Moines not to be places where people will fight for social change. They want people like Mark Curtis to quit moving to Des Moines to look for a job.

"But on that they will fail. They want workers in the packing industry, paperworkers, miners, workers of all kinds who will fight, to get the message that there are limits on your fighting."

The conflict over this frame-up has grown into something bigger than the ruling class was bargaining for, Barnes said. "There are two sides forming on a world scale. This truly will win or lose as an international battle in which the stakes are: Can this frame-up be gotten away with? Or will the attempt to do this to working people at this stage in history cost them more than it's worth?"

The ruling class didn't believe that the Curtis defense effort would be able to rally, in a unified way, workers, farmers, Blacks, Latinos, women, elected officials, socialists, communists, and religious figures.

They also misjudged the Socialist Workers Party and Young Socialist Alliance, Barnes said, assuming the socialists would simply view defending Curtis as their own fight, which others could support. "But I think we have found out something in this fight," Barnes emphasized. "Mark is *part* of all these supporters. Fellow workers in New Caledonia, fighters in Central America, miners in Nottinghamshire turn to Mark as a brother, as one of them."

Barnes concluded by explaining that if the international defense effort continues and increases, "There is no way on earth they will succeed in their goal. They will not put Mark Curtis in prison for twenty-five years. They will not get him down on his knees.

"They will not prevent him from continuing to be the same person he is today, fighting for the same things, believing the same deeply held convictions, saying them openly to the entire world. He will continue to do all this, no matter where he finds himself, for however long.

"And if we can believe that, we know it's our obligation and our opportunity to fight in the same way. To use the language they indicted Mark for, *Unidos venceremos!* [United we will win]."

Evidence of beating not allowed

Curtis in fact did not receive a fair trial. The court demanded that he prove his innocence, not that the prosecution prove him guilty. On top of this, the judge prevented most of the key evidence in Curtis's defense from ever reaching the jury.

At the prosecutor's request, Judge Harry Perkins ruled even before the trial opened that any testimony about the fact that Curtis was beaten bloody by the Des Moines police was "irrelevant and immaterial" and could not be presented in court. Prosecutor Catherine Thune claimed that since the two cops who assaulted him at the police station were not the ones who made the arrest, the beating had nothing to do with the rape charges.

During the pretrial motions, defense lawyer Mark Pennington explained why testimony regarding the beating was directly relevant to the case. "Certainly we have a right to present evidence for the defense," Pennington said, and "Mark Curtis is going to testify that he was placed in an incriminating position by a Des Moines police officer. . . .

"Even though the fight and the beating that took place at the Des Moines Police Department was by officers other than [arresting] Officer [Joseph] Gonzalez," Pennington said, "I still think it is relevant to show the institutional bias towards Mark Curtis. If the jury is going to have to deliberate and weigh whether or not there was any chance that a Des Moines police officer may have deliberately placed Mr. Curtis in an incriminating position, shouldn't they then have the opportunity to listen to other evidence of institutional bias against Mr. Curtis, and the fact that he was beaten up at the police station afterward?"

In arguing that the beating was irrelevant, prosecutor Thune also said it would be addressed separately in the later trial of Curtis on charges that he had assaulted the two cops who had interrogated him. That second trial never took place, however, because the government backed off the charges.

FBI files barred from jury

Throughout the pretrial hearing and trial Judge Perkins stood by his policy of ruling out evidence demonstrating that a political frame-up by the Des Moines police was possible.

For example, Perkins withheld from the jury the evidence that Mark Curtis's name appeared in FBI files compiled during the spying and disruption operation against CISPES. In the pretrial hearing, Pennington argued, "Shouldn't the jury have the right to know that in fact in the past the FBI has felt that Mark Curtis is important enough to spend time, energy, and effort to track his whereabouts, to include him within their FBI surveillance and, in fact, to have received documents under the Freedom of Information Act from the FBI which indicate that Mark Curtis was certainly known to them because of his activities for CISPES and others? Shouldn't the jury be allowed to hear that evidence, Your Honor?"

Perkins responded, "We're going to try an assault upon a person that says he committed it, and a burglary, and I think that's the trial we're having. We're not going to be trying the FBI or Mark Curtis for other things that he may or may not have done."

Chief witness previously suspended for lying

During cross-examination at the trial, Pennington asked the chief prosecution witness—police officer Gonzalez—if he had once been suspended for "lying about the details of that incident that occurred while you were a police officer for the City of Des Moines." Before the cop could answer, Thune objected and asked to discuss the matter in the judge's chambers. Outside the presence of the jury, Perkins decided to "sustain the objection on the grounds of relevancy. I think it just opens up a whole Pandora's box of evidence."

At Pennington's request, Gonzalez was questioned in the judge's chambers for appeal purposes. He confirmed that he had been suspended for lying ten years earlier, but claimed he had lied "to protect an informant."

Actually, according to a report in the May 24, 1978, *Des Moines Register*, Gonzalez "was suspended for four days for using unnecessary force and 10 days for 'lying' about the details of the incident." In the "incident," Gonzalez, along with another cop, brutalized two youths—one of whom was arrested merely for an expired traffic warrant—and then lied to cover up what he and his partner had done. According to the assistant city attorney at the time, one of the young men suffered a head injury; the other was thrown around by the hair. The case did not become public until one of the youths won an out-of-court damages settlement two months later.

In an earlier hearing, Judge Anthony Critelli had refused to order the State of Iowa to produce Gonzalez's personnel files so the defense could see what other "incidents" were on his record.

As Pennington pointed out in Judge Perkins's chambers, the fact that Gonzalez "has been suspended for lying about an incident as a police officer . . . goes to his credibility and to his bias." The jury, however, was not allowed to consider this fact.

Many other aspects of Curtis's trial were not fair.

With the unmistakable aim of ensuring Curtis would spend a long time in prison, for example, prosecutors added on—at his arraignment a full month after his arrest—the charge of burglary in the first degree, which carries a twenty-five-year mandatory sentence. No one claimed Curtis stole anything; his mere presence at the home of the alleged victim was deemed "burglary" under Iowa statutes. The other charge against him, sexual abuse in the third degree, carries only a ten-year penalty. Prosecutors had initially charged Curtis with second-degree sexual assault, which would have required them to provide evidence that Curtis had a weapon or otherwise threatened the alleged victim with death or serious injury. The charge was reduced at Curtis's arraignment.

Not a jury of his peers

Opponents of Mark Curtis's defense campaign argue that because he is white and was convicted by twelve white jurors, he had a jury of his peers. But that is not the case.

Mark Curtis is a worker. Workers, especially those who are Black or Hispanic, have a very different set of experiences from those of the middle-class whites who composed the big majority of the jury in Curtis's trial. Working people are much more likely to have personal knowledge of police brutality and frame-ups. They are less likely to simply take the word of a cop over that of a worker, with no questions asked.

A few years after Curtis's trial, the Iowa Court of Appeals found that Polk County, which includes Des Moines, selects jurors by methods that "exclude the poor and therefore minorities." On June 26, 1992, the *Des Moines Register* reported that according to the Iowa Court of Appeals, "Polk County's practice of picking juries discriminates against blacks and systematically excludes them from the jury process."

The jury that reached a verdict of "guilty" against Curtis was not made up of his peers—there were no Blacks on the jury, and only one union member.

Moreover, the one Hispanic juror was removed by Judge Perkins despite defense objections. Just before the deliberations began, juror James Garcia said he didn't think he could be fair because he was familiar with two locations referred to in the trial—the United Mexican-American Community Center and Los Compadres bar.

"Such knowledge in no way disqualified Mr. Garcia from service upon the jury, nor could it constitute bias or prejudice to either the State of Iowa or the Defendant," Curtis's attorneys pointed out in a motion for a new trial following his conviction. "The removal of James Garcia was without cause, and the removal of the only juror with a Mexican-American background denied Defendant of a fair cross-section of the community and denied his right to a fair and impartial trial."

In an affidavit filed several weeks after the verdict, juror

Blanche Stockbauer stated she had not been convinced Curtis was guilty beyond a reasonable doubt. "Although I eventually voted guilty," she said, "it is my belief that Mark Curtis is not guilty of the crime charged. I did not know that, if I continued my vote of not guilty, a mistrial would occur, which would result in a new trial for Mr. Curtis.

"One juror expressed, during deliberations, that he had made his mind up about Mr. Curtis's guilt before the defense presented any evidence in this case," Stockbauer added.

A second report of possible jury misconduct—fraternization between one juror and the Morris family during the trial—was never investigated.

No credible evidence
Despite all of the facts that were not allowed into the courtroom, many of those who attended the trial were convinced that the government did not have any credible evidence against Curtis.

"I was surprised by the verdict" of guilty on both counts, Nellie Berry told *Militant* reporter Margaret Jayko soon after the trial. Berry said she had tried to listen to the evidence presented as if she knew nothing of the case beforehand and had concluded that, given the number of gaps in the prosecution's case, a guilty verdict "was almost impossible." But Robert Berry, Nellie's husband, said he wasn't surprised. "I know the judicial system," he said. "Innocent people are even executed." Both Robert and Nellie Berry are longtime antiwar and political activists in Des Moines who first heard of Curtis's case at a demonstration against U.S. war moves in Central America.

Julia Terrell was Curtis's neighbor. "My first reaction" after hearing he had been arrested on rape charges, Terrell said, was, "What do we have across the street from us?"

Then she saw how badly Curtis had been beaten by the cops and "knew something was terribly wrong.

"I thought he was innocent by the time the trial started," Terrell said. "By the time the trial was over I *knew* he was innocent."

8

What the trial brought to light

Dozens of people filled the Polk County Courthouse in Des Moines, Iowa, September 7, 1988, to observe the trial of Mark Curtis. Among the crowd were unionists and farmers, civil rights activists and clergy. Some already supported the fight against the political frame-up of the young union activist and socialist. Others weren't sure, but were suspicious of the cops' story.

The prosecution's first witness was sixteen-year-old Demetria Morris. She testified that on March 4, 1988, she was sexually assaulted on the front porch of her house.

Morris said she and her brother Jason answered a knock at the door that evening from a man who said his name was Mark. She opened the door, thinking it might be her brother Mark, but instead found a stranger who asked for an address a few doors down the street. While she was talking to this man, she said, her brother went back inside the house. Morris stated that when she told the stranger to go look for the house he wanted, he pushed open the door to the enclosed front porch where she was standing, told her he had a knife, and attempted to rape her. In court she

YVONNE HAYES

Defense attorney Mark Pennington addressing jury during trial, September 1988.

swore that man was Mark Curtis.

There was no physical evidence, however, to back up Morris's claim that Curtis had assaulted her. The young woman described a lengthy attack on the front porch floor, which was covered with dirt, leaves, and dog hair. From the way she said the attacker wrestled with her, one would expect to find evidence of contact with the floor on the clothing of both individuals. Morris's sweatshirt, jeans, and underwear did have dirt and dog hair on them, and there were dried leaves in her hair. But no evidence of leaves or dog hair was found on Curtis's clothing.

Paul Bush, a forensic analyst for the Iowa Division of Criminal Investigation, examined the clothing of both Morris and Curtis. He found no seminal fluid on the clothing of either one and no exchange of pubic hairs. "As far as sexual contact is concerned, I found no seminal fluid or hairs to tie the two individuals together," Bush told the jury.

In addition to the absence of physical evidence linking Curtis to the crime of which he was accused, there were numerous contradictions in the testimony of Morris, her brother, and the two cops who arrested Curtis.

Curtis had alibi for time of assault

The most important flaw in the prosecution's case was that Curtis had an uncontested alibi for the time the young woman insisted the attack began.

Morris said the knock on the door came five minutes after she answered a telephone call from a stranger. At both her pretrial deposition and the trial, Morris testified this phone call came just as the television show "Video Soul" was starting. This show usually started at 7:30 P.M., she said. According to the broadcaster's program log, the show actually started at 8:00 P.M. on March 4, which would place the time of the attack between 8:05 P.M. and 8:10 P.M.

But Brian Willey, a co-worker of Curtis at the Swift packinghouse, testified that he was with Curtis from 7:00 to 8:30 that night in a crowded bar, Los Compadres. They shared a pitcher of beer with a third Swift worker and discussed the arrest of the workers at the plant a few days earlier, the work stoppage that afternoon, and the meeting protesting the immigration raid that Curtis had just attended. Willey said he was sure Curtis left at 8:30 "because I had to meet some people at nine o'clock so I kept looking at my watch."

Under Iowa law, this unrebutted alibi testimony by itself was sufficient grounds for acquittal. Judge Perkins, however, ruled against a defense motion to instruct the jury on the issue of alibi.

Description did not match Curtis

Morris's description of the man she says assaulted her did not match Curtis. The young woman insisted, for instance, that her attacker wore a belt—she saw and heard him unbuckle it. But Curtis was not wearing a belt that evening, and the cops did not find one during their investigation. She was also certain the assailant had smoker's breath. Curtis was an adamant nonsmoker, as witnesses who knew him testified.

Just a couple of hours after the alleged assault, Morris was examined at a local hospital. She told the doctor there that the man who attacked her was about five feet, six inches tall—just a couple of inches taller than herself—and wore a tan jacket. Curtis is more than six feet tall and was wearing a burgundy jacket. By the time she gave a deposition in May, Morris had changed her description to better match Curtis. At the trial, the young woman said, "Mark Curtis is kind of like almost the same height as my dad, and my dad's around six-two or six-three."

Supporters of the prosecution's case have argued that these discrepancies should be ignored because Morris was too traumatized to give a coherent story March 4. But when the prosecutor asked Jane Brackney, who helped examine Morris at the hospital, "Was she . . . able to relate in general what happened to her?" the nurse responded, "Yes, she could very well."

Curtis never saw Demetria Morris

While the assault was allegedly taking place, Jason Morris testified, he called the 911 emergency line and told a police dispatcher a man was raping his sister. A call was placed from the Morris house at 8:51 P.M., according to the dispatcher's computer records, about forty minutes later than Demetria Morris testified she had been attacked.

The call, in fact, was placed just about the time Mark Curtis arrived at the Morris house. After leaving Los Compadres bar at 8:30 P.M., he went home briefly, made the 8:45 call to Jackie Floyd to ask her to look out for his guests, and left for the store. Myung Kim told the jury she and her husband, Kevin Magee, had indeed made arrangements to stay over at Curtis's house after attending the Rural Women's Conference that evening. They had planned to arrive around 9:00 P.M.

Curtis testified that while he was driving to the store, a young woman—not Demetria Morris—came up to his car and asked him to drive her home because a man was after her. He agreed and drove her to the house that turned out to be the Morris home. He parked directly in front and, at the woman's request, waited on the porch while she checked to make sure the house was safe. A few moments later, Curtis said, "I heard a noise behind me, a 'bam' as the door flew open. . . . The first thing that went through my head was this was the guy who was after her." But it was the police.

"One of them grabbed me by the arm and said, 'I've got him,'" Curtis continued. "At this point I thought that there might be a misunderstanding here, that in fact she had called the police, worried about this guy who was after her, and that the police officers thought that I was the guy."

The cop walked Curtis into the back bedroom of the house. "He handcuffed me, my wrists behind my back," the activist testified, "sat me down on this bed that was there, he pushed me back onto the bed, and he unbuckled my pants and pulled them down."

Curtis said he never saw Demetria Morris that night. The first time he saw her was almost three months later at the Polk County Courthouse, where she gave a deposition accusing him of attacking her.

Contradictions in cops' testimony

Des Moines police officers Joseph Gonzalez and Richard Glade claim they arrived at the Morris house thirty to ninety seconds after the police dispatcher called them. The cops' and the young woman's versions of what happened next differ in some important facts.

When the two cops banged on the door, they both told the court, Morris ran out wearing only a sweatshirt and said she had just been raped. In her own testimony, however, the young woman insisted she had said nothing to the cops when they first got there. And the notes of the doctor who examined her indicate she had initially said she was not wearing her shirt when the cops arrived.

Gonzalez testified that as he came onto the porch he saw Curtis trying to pull up his pants while running toward the back of the house. The cop said he chased Curtis through the house and handcuffed him as he stood facing a bed in the back room. Glade, on the other hand, told the jury he saw Gonzalez handcuffing Curtis as he lay face down on the floor in the bedroom. Morris claimed she went into the bedroom and saw Curtis sitting on the bed with his penis exposed. Both of the cops said that would have been impossible.

Curtis was not allowed to fasten his pants before he was taken to the police station; he had to hold them up from behind while handcuffed.

"Did you want other officers to see that his pants were unfastened?" defense attorney Mark Pennington asked Gonzalez.

"No, I did not," answered the cop.

"That's what happened though, wasn't it?" said the lawyer. "You don't think that makes it more believable if his pants were down, the fact that they weren't fastened and he's holding them up with his handcuffed hands in back of him?"

Gonzalez replied, "The only persons that could have seen it were the officers that took him to the station." Those two

What Mark Curtis did on March 4, 1988

At the September 7–9, 1988, trial of Mark Curtis on charges of sexual abuse and burglary, the alleged victim testified that on the evening of March 4, 1988, when one of her favorite television shows had just begun, a man called on the telephone asking for Bonita, Denise, or Keith. The show began at 8:00 p.m. She told the caller that her parents, Denise and Keith Morris, weren't home.

Five or ten minutes later, she testified, a man knocked on the door, asking for the same people; she opened the door, started talking to him, and he proceeded to sexually assault and beat her until the police arrived. She said the man who did this was Mark Curtis. Below is a chronology, constructed from eyewitness evidence presented at the trial, of what Mark Curtis did that day and where he was at the time the alleged rape took place.

7:00 A.M. Curtis leaves home for work at Swift packinghouse in Des Moines.

2:00 P.M. Several Swift workers walk off production line to protest management decision to not allow them to go to 2:00 p.m. meeting to protest in-plant arrest three days earlier of seventeen Latino workers by immigration cops. Line stopped for ten minutes.

4:45 P.M. Curtis gets off work for the day.

5:00 P.M. Meeting at United Mexican-American Community Center to protest arrest of Swift 17. Curtis speaks at meeting, in Spanish, about need to involve the union at Swift, United Food and Commercial Workers Local 431, in fight to defend these workers. The meeting approved a call for a demonstration March 12 to protest arrests.

7:00 P.M. Curtis arrives at Los Compadres bar and restaurant after Swift 17 protest meeting. Talks to two co-workers from Swift about the meeting and plans for the following week's protest.

8:30 P.M. Curtis leaves Los Compadres, drives home.

8:40–8:45 P.M. Curtis calls friend Ellen Whitt and leaves message on her answering machine that he's going out for a few minutes and could she please let two friends of his who are coming over into her house if they show up before he gets back. Tells her that he is going to the store to buy food to cook dinner for people attending Militant Labor Forum the next night. Since Whitt isn't home, he calls neighbor Jackie Floyd and tells her the same thing.

8:45–8:50 P.M. Curtis leaves house to go to Hy-Vee grocery store. Woman stops Curtis at traffic light on corner of Clark and Harding, five blocks from his house, and asks for ride home because a man is chasing her. Curtis gives her lift to what turns out to be the house of the Morris family. She asks him to wait on the porch while she goes inside.

8:51 P.M. Police say they receive a 911 emergency call from someone whispering that his sister is being raped on the porch.

8:52 P.M. Police testify they dispatch car to house.

8:53 P.M. Police officer Joseph Gonzalez testifies cops arrive within 30–90 seconds. According to Curtis, a minute or two after he walks up to porch, cops arrive and burst onto porch. Gonzalez grabs Curtis, handcuffs him, pulls down his pants, and arrests him. Cops take keys to Curtis's car, where he had left flyers for event protesting government attacks on democratic rights.

officers, Charles Wolf and Daniel Dusenbery, were the ones who beat Curtis at the jail an hour or two later.

No history of violence toward women

In addition to the factual discrepancies in the testimony of witnesses for the prosecution, the government could not make a politically convincing case against Mark Curtis either.

Several people who knew Curtis well, both personally and through political collaboration, including his wife, Kate Kaku, testified at the trial that he had never carried out any act of violence or abusive behavior toward women, Blacks, or anyone else. Witnesses also spoke of Curtis's honesty and integrity.

One of those called in Curtis's defense was Ellen Whitt, who has a degree in psychology and experience working with women who have suffered sexual and physical abuse. In 1988 Whitt worked at the Swift packinghouse with Curtis and was also involved in the fight against the immigration raid there.

"Based on your knowledge of Mark Curtis, both socially and through your shared goals," Pennington asked her, "do you have any concern that Mark Curtis may harbor some type of animosity, propensity towards violence?"

"No," Whitt answered. "I've never seen any indication of it. . . . I know at least one occasion where some workers were threatening to beat up some of the Mexican workers at Swift and Mark intervened to tone that down and to explain to people how that would not be in the interest of the workers."

Jackie Floyd, who had known Curtis for three years through work in the Young Socialist Alliance, also testified. "Have you ever seen any example, any hint that somehow he might harbor some animosity towards women?" Pennington asked her.

"Never," said Floyd, who lived next door to Curtis until soon before the trial. "One of my two children is a girl. I have two kids, a son and a daughter, and they had become quite good friends of Mark and his wife."

"Do you have any concerns about your daughter, a young Black girl, being with Mr. Curtis?" asked the lawyer.

"Definitely not," she replied.

Lack of any motive

"They couldn't find anybody that could contradict the character testimony," said Pennington in an interview shown in the video *The Frame-up of Mark Curtis*, made by Hollywood director Nick Castle. The best the prosecution could come up with was that Curtis had made a false statement about his work experience on an application for a job in Birmingham, Alabama, during the recession of the early 1980s.

"The fact that the state of Iowa was able to obtain information concerning a false statement in an application for a former job in the state of Alabama tells me a great deal," Curtis's lawyer commented in the video interview. "It certainly tells me that they spent a great deal of time and effort and money to try and find out what they could concerning Mark Curtis's background, and shows they came up short."

The prosecution lacked any plausible explanation of why a young political activist, in the middle of an important union struggle, would go to a house where he knew no one and rape a fifteen-year-old who answered the door, knowing her brother was present. So the prosecution implied that Curtis arrived at the Morris house by accident, looking for the home of a drug dealer who had just moved in a few doors down. Prosecutor Thune put the girlfriend of the alleged dealer on the stand at the end of the trial. She said that she used to live across the street from Curtis, that she recognized him but had not known his name, and

STU SINGER

Director Nick Castle interviewing Curtis at Iowa Men's Reformatory in Anamosa for documentary film *The Frame-Up Of Mark Curtis*.

that she and her boyfriend might have spoken briefly with him in passing.

In all their investigations, however, the cops and the prosecutor's office could not find a single shred of evidence that Curtis ever had anything to do with drugs. His organization, the Socialist Workers Party, is well-known among political activists for the fact that its members do not use illegal drugs. This policy helps protect the party from police and employer victimization.

Frame-up needs no conspiracy theory

The prosecutor attempted to discredit any idea that Mark Curtis was framed up by arguing that such a possibility necessitated a far-fetched and complex conspiracy involving several people.

But Curtis and his supporters never claimed the cops had an elaborate scheme to nail the political activist. When Gonzalez pulled down Curtis's pants, creating evidence for other officers to see, that was the beginning of a frame-up of the kind hundreds of workers face every day when they are picked up and charged at the whim and convenience of the cops, prosecutors, and courts. Once the police searched Curtis's car and found leaflets showing his support for the fights of Blacks and immigrants, they certainly knew he was a political activist. When a short time later the cops called Curtis a "Mexican lover, just like you love those coloreds," it was clear the frame-up was political.

What's more, Curtis never claimed the young woman who accused him was part of a conspiracy. At one point Thune asked him, "When Demetria testified that you were the person that raped her, she's lying?"

"I heard her here," Curtis replied, "like we all did, and I believe something may have happened to her, maybe even what she said. But I was not that person and she is wrong about that much."

Immediately after Curtis's conviction, Pennington filed a motion for a new trial, based on the numerous abuses during the trial. Perkins ruled against the motion on November 18, 1988, just before sentencing Curtis to twenty-five years in prison.

In a final statement before the sentence was read, Curtis told the court, "Since my arrest back in March many thousands of people from around this state, from Des Moines, from the Philippines to New Zealand, have stood up and protested this frame-up of me and this railroad job, which is what it is.

"What happened to me is not that unique or unusual

compared to what many people around this country face. *The State of Iowa v. Mark Curtis* is not about rape or about burglary. . . . It's about the fear of jail and the fear of the billy club that they want to put in the hearts of working people.

"I'm going to keep on being part of the fight for working people no matter where I'll be," he continued. "My case is unusual only in one respect, and that is . . . the thousands of people who have stood up for my defense, and that is going to grow and I will be free in any case."

9

Behind bars but not out of politics

"The schools and big-business media, the politicians, and the churches teach people to look at prisoners as scum of the earth. But we're almost all working-class people, human beings with an interest in fighting for human rights," said Mark Curtis, explaining what a socialist worker does behind bars. "We have common interests, and the only way we're going to protect our rights is by our actions and our unity."

Sitting in the visiting yard of the John Bennett Correctional Center at the state penitentiary in Fort Madison, Iowa, in the summer of 1993, Curtis described the many people he had met in prison since beginning to serve his time in late 1988.

"I've met meatpackers and truck drivers, some who've been involved in union fights," he said. "There are veterans from [the U.S. wars in] Panama and Vietnam, and many people who've been touched by the civil rights movement. I met one guy who had fled the regime in El Salvador. He actually got his case overturned, because the trial was conducted in English—a language he didn't know."

Curtis explained one of the biggest challenges prisoners face is that "we have to keep in contact with the outside."

This isn't easy. The prison system is designed to cut inmates off from the rest of the world and discourage them from looking beyond the prison walls to broader struggles.

Attempts to isolate prisoners

Soon after his conviction, Curtis ran into some of the hundreds of rules and regulations used to accomplish this when the administration at the Iowa State Men's Reformatory in Anamosa refused to allow him to receive literature and letters in languages other than English. A subscription to the Spanish-language socialist magazine *Perspectiva Mundial* was denied. A Spanish/English dictionary sent him by the Mark Curtis Defense Committee was also rejected.

"It wasn't just me—they were denying other people that kind of thing too," Curtis noted. "One guy from Cambodia was trying to get letters from his family, and they wouldn't let him receive them."

The defense committee helped mount a campaign against the language rule. The prison warden was flooded with hundreds of letters protesting prison officials' refusal to allow Curtis to get the Spanish-language material. The fight was covered in Iowa newspapers, and eventually the administration backed off and allowed him to receive the literature.

"But they were still denying others their rights," Curtis said. "Other inmates used my protest letters, and many won their cases." When Curtis returned to the prison in Anamosa a couple years later, however, he noted that the authorities had "gone back to their old ways. They have so many rules to prevent prisoners from sharing books, passing a newspaper around, or sharing other things. One guy

Andile Yawa, a leader of the African National Congress Youth League, visiting Mark Curtis at John Bennett Correctional Center in Fort Madison, Iowa.

got in trouble for having a copy of the *Militant* that wasn't his," Curtis noted.

From within the prison walls, Curtis "tried to participate in different battles in the class struggle," mostly through the mail. The jailed unionist sent letters of support to machinists on strike against Eastern Airlines, coal miners in Britain, the United Farm Workers of Washington State, striking steelworkers at Trinity Industries in Bessemer, Alabama, and others.

Curtis also wrote to victims of police brutality and political prisoners around the world, including Native American activist Leonard Peltier, fighters for Irish independence, and Rodney King, whose videotaped beating by the Los Angeles cops in March 1991 sparked worldwide outrage. "Me and another inmate wrote to Tim Anderson," Curtis said. Anderson is a political activist and supporter of Aboriginal rights in Australia who was framed up on murder charges. "And I've been sent letters from prisoners in Turkey, Arizona, Texas, New Jersey, and many other places," he added. "I'm not allowed to receive those. I just get a notice from the mail room that they came." Prison authorities make sure that inmates from different institutions and parts of the world cannot communicate with each other.

Visits from other political fighters are part of how Curtis kept in touch with the rest of the world. In 1992, for example, he met with Andile Yawa, a leader of the African National Congress Youth League. "That visit was a big thing. Other inmates asked me to pass along questions about the struggle in South Africa, and some still ask me what's happening there." A visit from James Warren, the Socialist Workers Party candidate for U.S. president in the 1992 election, drew interest from other prisoners as well. Curtis was one of the national chairpeople of the election campaign.

"The weekly meeting I have with members of the SWP branch in Des Moines is probably the most important," Curtis said. "We always include an educational discussion, usually on an article out of the *Militant*. And we discuss what else is happening in politics, as well as my defense campaign."

In the 1993 interview, Curtis described a typical day for him in prison: "I work full time in the printshop here" for about fifty cents an hour. "After work I exercise, spend time talking with people, have dinner. In the evening I do a lot of reading. And I set aside time to study Spanish." He pointed to how Nelson Mandela, Fidel Castro, James P. Cannon, and other revolutionary leaders who have gone to prison used that time to study and learn. "They're good examples of what to do in prison," he said. "That's why the fight for literature is so important."

Martin Luther King Jr. Organization

Soon after his incarceration at the Anamosa prison, Curtis joined the Martin Luther King Jr. Organization, a group of "inmates interested in the civil rights movement and fighting for better conditions in prison," as he put it. He was elected secretary of the group until prison authorities removed him from that position.

Curtis described the first meeting of the organization he attended in January 1989. "They had an open microphone. The bombing of Libya [by the U.S. military] had happened not long before. So I spoke about that, about how Martin Luther King had spoken against the U.S. war in Vietnam, and about how the fight against racism has to be tied to events in the world. I got a very good response." The group brought in outside speakers and kept a library of political books. One order of literature from Pathfinder Press was held up by the prison administration. After many protests, the Martin Luther King Jr. Organization was able to win the release of the books.

"The books by Malcolm X and Thomas Sankara were popular," Curtis said, "and so were those by Karl Marx and Frederick Engels. The copy of the *Communist Manifesto* was checked out a lot."

A few months after the group won the right to receive the books, the prison administration decided to transfer Curtis to the penitentiary in Fort Madison because, one prison report said, he was building "a power base" at Anamosa. Curtis's transfer came after he, with the help of other inmates, had waged an unsuccessful fight against a disciplinary report for supposedly betting on the Super Bowl. He was also written up for spitting on the pavement during a basketball game. The transfer "was their admission that they couldn't stop me from talking to people and influencing them," Curtis commented.

Curtis was sent back to Anamosa in August 1991. That time he and three other prisoners started a study group on socialism. "We started with the *Communist Manifesto*," he said. "We scrounged up several copies and took turns leading the class." Before they got a chance to read more books, however, Curtis was transferred back to Fort Madison.

Discussions about world politics

Prisoners have the same kinds of discussions about politics and world events as workers in a packinghouse or auto factory, Curtis noted. Leading up to the Gulf War in late 1990 and early 1991, for instance, "there was a lot of sentiment against the buildup." Several inmates signed a letter to the *Des Moines Register* opposing Washington's war moves. Once the bombing started in mid-January and U.S. troops were engaged in combat, he said, most prisoners shifted to a position of support, albeit grudging, for the U.S. war.

The Pathfinder book *U.S. Hands Off the Mideast!* "really helped," Curtis said. "One prisoner who had read it began to argue with another who supported the war, 'Hey, you've got to read this. We're being pushed into cheerleading something we shouldn't.'"

Curtis also had numerous discussions with other inmates about the U.S. government's embargo against Cuba. Like growing numbers of people throughout the United States, more prisoners are expressing the view that the embargo should end. "People ask me questions about Cuba," Curtis said. "'Do people have freedom to express themselves?' 'What are prisons like there?' 'Why do people come here from Cuba?'"

Curtis wrote in the *Militant* about many of the discussions and struggles at the prisons where he's been. He and John Flowers, who is Sioux, wrote about the fight of Native American inmates in Anamosa to be allowed to practice their religion and culture.

Curtis also contributed articles on many other political questions. He and another inmate at Fort Madison coauthored a 1991 article for the *Militant* condemning the government for chipping away at the right of women to choose abortion. "He approached me about doing the article, because it was an issue he felt strongly about. It reflects the authority the *Militant* has—a lot of people read it."

Fighting the frame-up from inside

Other prisoners at Fort Madison had various views about Curtis's defense campaign. "A lot of people are interested," Curtis said. "They like to see someone fighting back against the type of railroading that happened to me. When I won my lawsuit against the cops who beat me, they really liked that.

"Not everyone supports me, because of the nature of the [sexual abuse] charge," he added. "There are people who believe whatever the state says someone did. And some people don't like me being a communist. But most people judge you by what you do—if you take the inmates' side, join in fights, and stand up for what you believe, people respect you."

Referring to his struggle for justice, Curtis said, "No amount of pressure or threats will make me give up this fight. I've gotten support from working people, fighters, and supporters of democratic rights around the world. I haven't been worn down and I'm more confident than ever that I'll leave here stronger than when I came in."

HARRY RING   BLACK STAR\PETER TURNLEY

NAT LONDON

Curtis continued to discuss politics with fellow workers while in prison. (Counterclockwise from top left) High school students in California at 1994 rally against anti-immigrant Proposition 187; millions of workers and youth in France protest cuts to social wage and demand a shorter workweek in December 1995; the road from Kuwait City to Basra, Iraq, after massive U.S. bombing in February 1991.

10

Victory in lawsuit against cop beating

In May 1989 Curtis filed a federal lawsuit against the city of Des Moines and the cops who had beaten him in the city jail a little more than a year earlier. Curtis charged the cops and local officials with violating his constitutional rights to be free from unreasonable search and seizure, violence, and threats of violence while he was incarcerated; with cruel and unusual punishment; and with negligence and assault and battery.

On January 31, 1992, U.S. District Court judge Charles Wolle ruled in favor of the jailed unionist and socialist. Des Moines cops Charles Wolf and Daniel Dusenbery, who brutalized Curtis, were found guilty of battery and ordered to pay $11,000 in damages, plus costs and attorneys' fees. The judgment totaled $64,000. "There was no way the police could deny that he was injured and the only people that could have done it were the police," commented Alfredo Alvarez, former head of the Des Moines Human Rights Commission and a longtime supporter of Curtis's fight for justice.

But the obvious fact that the police had caused Curtis's injuries was no guarantee of a victory. Brutality at the hands of the cops is a stark reality for thousands of working people in cities and towns throughout the United States. Workers who are immigrants, Black, or Latino are especially likely to come under attack, as are those active in union struggles and social protest movements. Even on the all-too-rare occasions when cops are brought to trial for such brutal acts, they almost always claim their use of force was necessary and justified, just as they did in the case of Mark Curtis. And the courts generally take the word of the police.

More than the cops' guilt, it was an upturn in the struggle against police violence and racism, both in Des Moines and on a national level, that was essential to Curtis winning the lawsuit.

'That doesn't happen in Des Moines'

While Wolf and Dusenbery were beating Curtis on March 4, 1988, Stu Singer was trying to get him out of jail. When

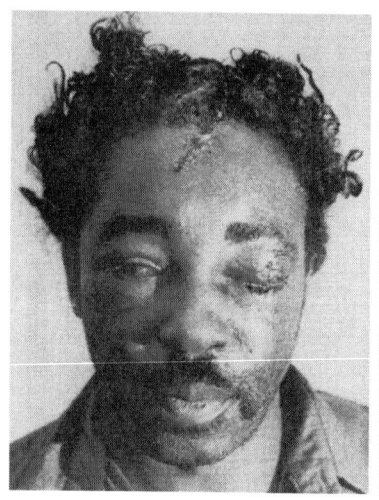 

THE REGISTER/KAREN MITCHELL   CHRIS REMPLE

After Larry Milton (left) was beaten by police in December 1991 thousands protested against cop brutality. Right: February 1992 hearing on police brutality called by Des Moines City Council.

officials at the city jail gave him the runaround about whether they had Curtis in custody, Singer, who had some experience in the civil rights and labor movements, became concerned the cops might be beating him. But virtually all the lawyers and political activists he spoke to that night, Singer said, told him not to worry—that kind of thing didn't happen in Des Moines.

Over the next few years, however, it became clear to many people that racism, sexual harassment, and brutality are standard practice among cops in that Iowa city.

A report issued by the Des Moines Civil Service Commission in November 1988 detailed widespread racist and sexist abuse within the police department. The *Des Moines Register* reported on the conclusions of the investigation, which reinstated a female police officer who had been fired for protesting racist remarks made by her superior. "The police department's internal investigation lacked credibility," the *Register* said. "The internal investigators tried to 'clear the supervisor.'"

Four months earlier a former officer who had been sexually harassed by other cops for years won a discrimination lawsuit against the police department. Testimony in that case revealed not only sexist but also racist harassment. Two white cops, for example, had donned Ku Klux Klan garb to "welcome" a Black officer onto the squad.

The Des Moines cops have also become well-known for beating people in their custody. The police were forced to install a camera in the elevator at the city jail that is used to transport suspects from the booking area to the holding cells. The "elevator ride" had become the target of a growing outcry against police beatings. Both Wolf and Dusenbery had either shot or beaten people in their custody before Curtis's arrest.

"We do know these beatings occur," Alvarez told the Civil Service Commission in May 1988.

Rally in Des Moines to celebrate January 1992 victory in Curtis's lawsuit against cops who beat him.

The beating of Larry Milton

On December 28, 1991, Des Moines police brutally beat Larry Milton, provoking an explosion of anger against police violence, especially in the Black community. Cops struck the thirty-five-year-old Black man repeatedly on the head with a heavy metal flashlight in front of dozens of witnesses, after they had cuffed both his hands and feet. It took twenty-two metal staples to close his gaping head wounds.

The attack on Milton occurred while the graphic videotaped image of Los Angeles police beating Rodney King was still fresh in people's minds.

"No excuse" became the slogan of thousands of people who participated in protest meetings, public hearings, and radio call-in shows to denounce police brutality. Many came forward with their own stories of cop violence meted out to themselves or people they know. One woman recounted how all three of her sons had been assaulted by the Des Moines police.

Curtis and twenty-four other prisoners at the John Bennett Correctional Center in Fort Madison, Iowa, wrote to Milton expressing their solidarity.

The police and their political backers responded to the public outcry by launching a campaign to slander Milton and justify their actions. In arguments strikingly similar to those made by the cops in Los Angeles to justify beating King, the police sergeant in charge of the assault on Milton claimed he was drunk, on drugs, and did not seem to be affected by repeated blows to the head.

Despite all the protests, a grand jury eventually refused to indict the cops who beat Milton.

'Standard operating procedure'

During the trial of Wolf and Dusenbery, Des Moines police chief William Moulder sought to prove that the two cops had acted properly in beating Curtis by introducing as evidence the police department's Uniform Division Standard Operating Procedures. The manual offers tips to cops on how to use force against suspects. One section, titled "Attacking vital body points," suggests twenty-one body parts that police should target: "Eyes—gouge, throw items; . . . Neck—nearly all neck vital for strike, pinch or choking; . . . Kidneys—strike inwards; . . . Groin—strike or kick."

"Public relations—when possible, avoid force in front of public audience," the manual advises. "When not possible, attack hard and quick."

These standard operating procedures introduced by Moulder actually ended up shining a spotlight on a little corner of the truth: that what happened to both Mark Curtis and Larry Milton was not some aberration but part of the cops' routine work.

At the height of the public debate, protests, and demonstrations against the beating of Larry Milton, Curtis's lawsuit came before Judge Wolle in January 1992. Wolle ended up ruling that cops "Wolf and Dusenbery both knew they were using excessive force when they kneed [Curtis] in the eye and groin while he was lying on the floor on his back, unable to flee or cause them harm."

"This is a big victory, not just for me, but for all victims of police brutality," Curtis declared when the ruling came down.

Leaders of the fight against police brutality in Des Moines were among those who addressed a February 8, 1992, rally there to celebrate the outcome of the suit. "I am ecstatically happy for the victory for Mark Curtis," said Dudley Allison, one of the leaders of the anti–police brutality fight. "What this does, in my opinion, is open the door for the prosecution of the officers that commit these types of crimes."

Also addressing the rally were Sonja Palmer, who founded Mothers and Wives Against Police Brutality after the Milton beating, and Ako Abdul Samad, a member of the board of directors of a Black community radio station central in demanding justice for Milton.

Greg McCartan, a leader of the Socialist Workers Party, said, "This ruling by a federal judge goes right to the heart of Mark's frame-up trial. . . . If a federal judge rules that the cops lied about beating Mark, then the cop who testified against him could have been lying as well."

The ruling "means many more people will be willing to join the call for [Curtis's] immediate release," Kate Kaku, a leader of the defense effort, pointed out. "We think the day of Mark's release has been brought closer and it will be helped by what we do now with this latest victory."

11

The fight to free Mark Curtis

As a concerned unionist I am writing you in behalf of the request of Mark Curtis for immediate parole consideration.
> GEORGE LACH
> Fifth vice president
> American Federation of
> State, County, and Municipal
> Employees Local 2203
> Baltimore, Maryland

Please release Mark Curtis from jail as soon as possible. He did not rape or rob anyone, but was a victim of a police frame-up for his defense of the rights of immigrant workers.
> ARTHUR WALTERS
> Associate professor
> University of Medicine
> and Dentistry of New Jersey

If Mark Curtis admitted his guilt, would he be free now? I understand Mr. Curtis has served enough time (five years) to be released from his ten year sexual abuse charge.
> DAVID OSTERBERG
> Representative,
> Iowa state legislature

ARGIRIS MALAPANIS

IRENE SOSA

Top: explaining case at November 1994 world meeting in solidarity with Cuba, held in Havana. Below: activists learning about frame-up at abortion rights demonstration in Washington, D.C., April 1989.

I write not only to show my solidarity with a fellow political prisoner but to support his request for an early parole.

> BRENDAN DONAGHY
> Irish independence fighter
> jailed in Northern Ireland

These letters were among hundreds presented to the Iowa Board of Parole on behalf of Mark Curtis in September and October of 1993. In the years following Curtis's incarceration in 1988, thousands of people around the world called on the parole board to release him.

Those who supported Curtis's parole over the years included civil rights activist Coretta Scott King, Detroit mayor Coleman Young, civil liberties attorney William Kunstler, Peruvian political activist and politician Hugo Blanco, South African activist and former political prisoner Fred Dube, the General Confederation of Labor in France, and numerous others.

The jailed unionist and socialist had a strong case for parole. He met the state's usual criteria—good conduct in prison, strong support outside, and several job offers. He had already served out the sentence on the sexual abuse charge. (Under Iowa law, which reduces the sentence by one day for each day of "good time" served, a prisoner is usually released after serving half their term—five years of a ten-year sentence in Curtis's case.) He remained in jail only on the phony burglary charge.

Nevertheless, the Iowa Board of Parole refused to even give Curtis a hearing in 1993. The obstacles he faced in winning parole reflected both the political nature of the case and the curtailment of democratic rights of prisoners in general.

Parole Now! campaign

As time went by, Curtis's case for parole became more compelling. New people were drawn to support his fight for free-

Frankie Travis addressing October 1994 rally in Des Moines to demand Curtis's release. Travis, a "road warrior" from United Paperworkers International Union Local 7837, fought lockout by A.E. Staley Company in Decatur, Illinois.

dom as it became obvious that his continued incarceration was the result of a pattern of political prejudice against him on the part of Iowa government and prison authorities.

Many people who were outraged at the obviously discriminatory treatment Curtis received in prison became open to seeing, after a review of the facts, that he was convicted on trumped-up charges in the first place, and that the government railroaded him because of his actions as a unionist and working-class fighter.

That's why the political campaign to press for parole was such an important part of the Mark Curtis Defense Committee's efforts. It aimed both to break the frame-up politically and to get Curtis out of prison, so he could more fully participate in political activity. It provided a way for Curtis's supporters to reach out broadly in the labor movement, to young people, among supporters of democratic rights, and to others to explain the facts of the frame-up and win new support.

In addition to the letters, a delegation of Curtis supporters attended each parole hearing on his case. The prison authorities and Iowa state parole board made clear they did not like this broad-based defense. "You have made this case a political circus," a parole board member said at one of the hearings. "You have done everything possible to make this appear a political issue and it's not." Supporters of Curtis who attended his hearings in 1990 and 1991 were searched by the prison's Correctional Emergency Response Team—something that was not done to those attending other inmates' hearings.

Those who supported the frame-up and wanted to keep Curtis in jail also focused on the parole board. Keith and Denise Morris, the parents of the woman Curtis supposedly attacked, attended the hearings, arguing vigorously against his release. The Workers League and a few individuals such as Mary Bertin, an official of the Boston NAACP chapter, also campaigned against any early release of Curtis.

While seeking broad public support in his fight for parole, Curtis also appealed to the Iowa and U.S. courts, pointing to the violations of his constitutional rights during the trial. All ruled against him, culminating in a January 1995 decision by a federal district appeals panel in St. Louis.

Sexual Offenders Treatment Program

One of the most blatantly undemocratic demands the Iowa Board of Parole put on Curtis was that he participate in a Sexual Offenders Treatment Program (SOTP) that requires admission of guilt.

This issue was first raised at Curtis's third parole hearing in November 1991. "Until you have been to the Sexual Offenders Treatment Program, you will get no consideration from this board," Barbara Binnie, one of three parole board members at that hearing, told Curtis. Chairman Walter Saur made similar statements, which were not contested by the third board member present.

Curtis consistently explained that he could not submit to the SOTP because he was innocent. The first item in the "criteria for program participation" reads, "Admit guilt—take responsibility for own crime."

At his 1992 hearing, Curtis asked whether there was any rule requiring prisoners to undergo the SOTP. "I don't know that it's a rule," Lorence said. "It is a policy, and we certainly recommend people engage in it. I can't say we absolutely have never paroled anyone who didn't go through the program," she added.

Requiring prisoners to go through such a program as a condition of parole is an attack on the right to presumption of innocence and freedom from self-incrimination.

A 1991 ruling by the Montana Supreme Court held that convicted sex offenders cannot be required to undergo therapy as a condition of staying out of prison if an essential part of the therapy is an acknowledgment of guilt. In that case Donald Imlay maintained his innocence on charges of sexually assaulting a child. He was convicted and sentenced to five years in prison. The court ruled that the sentence be suspended on the condition Imlay take part in a sexual therapy program. When he continued to deny the charges against him, Imlay was dropped from the program and incarcerated.

The Montana court said that under the Fifth Amendment the state cannot increase a sentence for refusal to confess to a crime and ordered a new sentencing. The U.S. Supreme Court allowed the ruling to stand.

Not voluntary, and truly degrading

Prison treatment programs like Iowa's SOTP are never truly voluntary, despite claims by the authorities. Inmates are always under pressure to go along with them in hopes of release or better treatment, whether the pressure is overt or not.

Sexual offenders' programs are becoming very widespread, according to Margaret Winter, a senior staff attorney with the American Civil Liberties Union's National Prison Project. In a 1993 interview she described a so-called treatment program in Vermont against which ACLU attorneys filed a class-action lawsuit. State officials claim the program is voluntary, Winter said. "But really it's only as voluntary as in Mark's case." She pointed to the example of a prisoner who gets a sentence of two to twenty years. "They say, 'If you do the program you may get out in two years, otherwise you'll be in for twenty,'" Winter explained.

These sexual offenders' programs, like many other "rehabilitation" schemes behind bars, attempt to demean and

SHIRLEY PEÑA

Supporters deliver letters to the parole board requesting Curtis's release, September 1995.

break prisoners. The Vermont system is a good illustration. According to Winter, participants are required to watch a range of pornographic materials while their degree of arousal is monitored. Prison officials claim information from such tests can be used to predict who is likely to commit a sex offense.

Inmates in the Vermont program are also forced to relate their "deviant fantasies" to a therapist, Winter said. Those who are paroled from the program often have to continue this treatment for years on an outpatient basis. Their parole can be, and sometimes is, revoked if the fantasies don't meet with the therapist's approval.

"A lot of people refuse to go through the program" and instead serve the time, Winter commented. "It's so degrading."

Iowa's SOTP relies on humiliating methods, too. Inmates in the program are required to participate in group "feedback" sessions where they are encouraged to berate each other for the crimes they were accused of committing. "The person receiving feedback will listen and not speak until all feedback is given," the SOTP rules read. "Eye contact will be kept at all times. . . . Retaliation for negative feedback will not be tolerated." SOTP participants must also write an essay titled "Through My Victim's Eyes," detailing the "happenings of the offense as the victim experienced it, written in first person."

Such "counseling" is supposed to help each prisoner "own your crime."

Until 1993 most prisoners in Iowa were entitled by law to an annual hearing before the parole board. New legislation changed that, leaving it up to the board to decide which inmates get the chance to present their case. The parole board used the new rule to deny a hearing to Curtis and many other prisoners.

"I should have been granted an immediate hearing," Curtis

said after the board's decision in October 1993. "Defenders of democratic rights need to insist that prisoners be allowed to argue themselves in front of the board." He pointed out that with the completion of the sexual abuse sentence—the only crime he was really accused of—it was harder than ever for the authorities to justify keeping him in prison.

Instead of granting him a hearing, the parole board said Curtis should be transferred to a prison hospital in Oakdale for psychological evaluation. After meeting with Curtis the psychologist recommended that there was no need for further psychological review. At the end of 1993, the Oakdale hospital rejected his transfer, writing that there were "no psychological issues" in his case.

Based on this, Curtis asked for a parole hearing and release; the board again rejected the request. He did, however, win a "gate pass"—permission to work outside the walls of the John Bennett Correctional Center. Such permission is considered a step on the road to minimum security and eventual release. Describing his new job as a janitor in the maximum security prison next door to Bennett, which he began in July 1994, Curtis said, "In spite of the hassles," such as being strip-searched before and after each shift, "it's a positive step. It demonstrates a small but real victory in the campaign for my defense and freedom."

A year in 'lockup'

Soon after, prison authorities put a new obstacle in the way of Curtis's release. At the end of August, he was thrown into investigative segregation in the maximum security unit. He was charged with assaulting another inmate. Curtis explained that while he had been in an argument, he never assaulted anyone.

In a column for the *Militant*, Curtis described the hearing he had before Administrative Law Judge Charles Harper.

The hearing was held in the lockup cell house. I was handcuffed behind my back and couldn't take notes or turn the pages of the written material they placed in front of me except with a not-very-successful contortionist maneuver. When I asked to at least be cuffed in front, my request was denied even though I already had leg shackles on and two guards were present. I also requested that my lawyer be present or at least that the hearing be postponed until I had a chance to meet with him. This too was denied.

Secret "evidence" against me, in the form of a "confidential informant" statement, was determined to be "reliable." The judge refused to let me know what it said or who said it, but he claimed it was an inmate eyewitness who saw me assault a guy who was awaiting an examination in the hospital outpatient area. The other evidence was a transcript of a recorded interview with a nurse who says she observed the alleged assault.

I denied assaulting anyone and pointed out that the nurse did not identify me at the time and that the transcript itself is mainly a statement from two guards, with one- or two-word responses by the nurse. It wasn't signed or initialed by anyone, and had a coached character to it. The judge admitted that the transcript was "not the best evidence," but that it would be used because it "corroborated" the confidential information.

On the basis of these proceedings, Curtis was sentenced to the maximum penalty allowed under prison regulations—thirty days solitary confinement "in the hole" and a year in "lockup."

This is a common form of punishment. According to a 1992 article in the *Des Moines Register*, nearly a third of the inmates in the maximum security unit of the Iowa State Penitentiary at Fort Madison are in lockup at any given time. They are confined to tiny cells — about five-and-a-half by eight feet — for twenty-three hours a day. They are allowed one hour of exercise a day Monday to Friday in chain-link and barbed-wire pens. The prisoners are limited to three ten-minute showers a week, and have to eat in their cells. Those who are "in the hole" are denied exercise time for ten days at a stretch, and lose other rights, such as having a radio in their cell. With lockup sentences stretching for months and years, some inmates go crazy from the isolation.

With frequent visits and many more letters from supporters, Curtis did keep in contact with the world, despite being in a "prison within prison." He increased the number of articles he wrote for the *Militant* during the 344 days he spent in lockup.

It was during the lockup sentence that Pathfinder published the first edition of this pamphlet, *Why Is Mark Curtis Still in Prison?* Iowa authorities at first refused to give Curtis the copy that had been sent to him. But two weeks later, with protest messages beginning to flood the warden's office, they reversed course.

As supporters got out the word about the blatantly discriminatory character of the lockup and Curtis's continued incarceration, new fighters were won to his defense. Unionists from central Illinois, where workers were on strike against the equipment manufacturer Caterpillar, tire maker Bridgestone/Firestone, and corn processor A.E. Staley, were among those who sent letters protesting the lockup and demanding parole. Roger Warren and Tim Bettger, two Canadian gold miners who were jailed on frame-up charges following a strike in Yellowknife, Northwest Territories, became staunch supporters of Curtis. The Movement of Rural Landless Workers in Brazil, a group that organizes land takeovers by landless peasants, took up the case. Some five thousand Brazilian peasants signed letters to the Iowa Board of Parole supporting Curtis's release.

In addition, forces who had stood firmly by the defense effort since the beginning, from civil rights activists in Iowa to communists in Cuba and militants of the African National Congress in South Africa, continued to express their support.

Victory in parole fight

When Curtis's case again came before the parole board for review in the fall of 1995, the state decided that keeping Curtis behind bars had become too politically costly for them. The longer the case dragged on, the easier it became for others to see it for what it was: a political victimization. Curtis was granted a parole hearing for the first time in three years. In the weeks leading up to the hearing, the board received some five hundred letters urging that Curtis be released.

The proceeding took place at the prison on November 21. A delegation of Curtis's supporters attended the hearing. In addition, reporters from the *Des Moines Register* and the *Militant* were present. For the first time members of the Morris family did not attend.

Curtis thanked the board for hearing his case and taking the time to review the letters of support, and then presented his request to be released. After the board members announced they would grant the parole, board member Walter Saur tried to downplay the impact of the letters. Gesturing to the delegation of supporters, he declared, "These people are not why you're getting out. . . . Don't count on these people, or more letters, to do anything." But this broad support was essential to Curtis's defense, as the whole fight up until that point, and the seven-month battle to actually win entry into the state of Illinois, proved.

Curtis was taken straight back to his cell after the parole hearing, without a chance to do more than give a thumbs-up sign. On his lunch break a couple hours later he telephoned the supporters who had attended the hearing. "This is a tremendous victory," he said. "I always knew this day would come, but it wouldn't have happened without all the people who wrote letters, showed up for parole hearings, sold pamphlets about my case, and campaigned for my release." He pledged to use this victory to rejoin others fighting for justice around the world.

NAOMI CRAINE

Supporters celebrate in Ft. Madison, Iowa, after parole board decision in November 1995 to release Curtis. (from left) Kitty Loepker, Frankie Travis, Kate Kaku, Suzanne Curtis, Hazel Zimmerman, Jane Curtis, Dannen Vance, John Studer, Norton Sandler, Natalie Bombaro, and Nick Castle.

Finances[1]

The fight for justice for Mark Curtis was made possible by thousands of donations from workers, farmers, youth, and others who saw this battle as their own. Over the eight years of its existence, the Mark Curtis Defense Committee raised $639,987 and spent $635,753.[2] At Curtis's request, the funds that remained when the committee closed its books in September 1996 were donated to the Political Rights Defense Fund, Inc., a nonpartisan organization with a more than twenty-year history defending those victimized by government and police agencies.

The majority of contributions were small—from one dollar to one hundred dollars. A total of $4,613 was donated by trade union locals. The Political Rights Defense Fund raised and contributed $66,612.

The two largest expenses were for outreach and legal fees. Outreach efforts included speaking tours by leaders of the defense effort across the United States and around

---

1. This chapter is summarized from a financial report prepared by John Studer and Chris Naper when the Mark Curtis Defense Committee was dissolved. Studer and Naper were the coordinator and treasurer, respectively, of the defense committee at that time. A copy of the complete report can be ordered from the Political Rights Defense Fund, P.O. Box 761, Church Street Station, New York, NY, 10007, or viewed, along with the rest of the Mark Curtis Defense Committee files, at the State Historical Society in Madison, Wisconsin.

2. All figures have been rounded off to the nearest dollar. The exact amounts are reported in the chart on page 90.

the world, promotional material explaining the fight, and mailings to support groups and individuals. Representatives of the defense campaign traveled to the Philippines and New Zealand; Denmark, Sweden, Norway, France, Britain, and other places in Europe; toured Mexico at the request of leaders of the Mexican Commission for the Defense and Promotion of Human Rights; and won support in Cuba and South Africa. A special tour was organized of the southern United States by civil rights leaders and others.

Legal expenses included the defense effort leading up to Curtis's trial in September 1988, appealing the conviction up to the U.S. Court of Appeals, Curtis's successful federal lawsuit against the Des Moines police for violating his civil rights by brutally beating him on the night of his arrest, and the legal defense against various attempts by Iowa authorities to victimize Curtis while he was in prison.

The committee also aided Curtis in taking on a series of pro-prosecution provocations launched against him in an effort to break him politically and destroy his defense committee. One such provocation was a lawsuit that claimed the defense committee was a fraud and that attempted to seize its funds and obtain the names of those who contributed to it. The committee was forced to hire attorneys to meet this attack. It ultimately won a court order protecting the privacy of its contributors.

The defense committee also helped cover some of Curtis's financial needs in prison, especially those that enabled him to maintain contact with the outside world. Among these were the purchase of books and newspaper subscriptions, a television set, a typewriter, paper, and postage.

Finally, the defense committee allocated funds to prepare its political and legal files for the State Historical Society in Madison, Wisconsin, where they are available for activists and researchers.

Mark Curtis Defense Committee
Financial Statement
March 5, 1988 to September 1, 1996

Income
    Contributions $368,077.22
    Rallies, tours, support groups   149,837.82
    Political Rights Defense Fund   66,612.84
    Loans   42,245.00
    Literature sales   13,214.29

    TOTAL INCOME $639,987.17

Expenses
    Outreach, travel, tours $161,524.78
    Legal fees   120,734.74
    Literature and materials   78,584.94
    Rent, utilities, office supplies   70,189.01
    Volunteer expenses   54,760.65
    Postage   49,575.41
    Loan repayment   42,245.00
    Telephone   37,271.75
    Prison expenses   18,476.84
    Bank charges   2,390.33

    TOTAL EXPENSES $635,753.45

    Balance as of September 1, 1996 $4,233.72*

---

* An additional $678.92 was spent preparing and delivering the defense committee files to the State Historical Society in Madison, Wisconsin. The remaining $3,554.80 was turned over, at Curtis's request, to the Political Rights Defense Fund.

from Pathfinder
MALCOLM X, BLACK LIBERATION AND THE ROAD TO WORKERS POWER

JACK BARNES

"Don't start with Blacks as an oppressed nationality. Start with the vanguard place of workers who are Black in broad, proletarian-led struggles in the US. From the Civil War to today, the historical record is mind-boggling. It's the strength and resilience, not the oppression, that bowls you over."—*Jack Barnes*

Drawing lessons from a century and a half of struggle, this book helps us understand why the revolutionary conquest of power by the working class will make possible the final battle for Black freedom—and open the way to a world based not on exploitation, violence, and racism, but human solidarity. A socialist world.

$20. Also in Spanish and French.

Companion volume to
THE CHANGING FACE OF U.S. POLITICS
Working-Class Politics and the Trade Unions

JACK BARNES

A handbook for working people seeking to build the kind of party needed to prepare for coming class battles through which we will revolutionize ourselves, our unions, and all society.

$24. Also in Spanish, French, and Swedish.

WWW.PATHFINDERPRESS.COM

EXPAND *Your Revolutionary Library*

Soldier of the Cuban Revolution
From the Cane Fields of Oriente to General of the Revolutionary Armed Forces
LUIS ALFONSO ZAYAS

The author recounts his experiences over five decades in the revolution. From a teenage combatant in the clandestine struggle and 1956–58 war that brought down the US-backed dictatorship, to serving three times as a leader of the Cuban volunteer forces that helped Angola defeat an invasion by the army of white-supremacist South Africa, Zayas tells how he and other ordinary men and women in Cuba changed the course of history and, in the process, transformed themselves as well. $18. Also in Spanish.

Washington's 50-year Domestic Contra Operation
LARRY SEIGLE

As the US rulers prepared to smash working-class resistance and advance their interests through the interimperialist slaughter of World War II, Washington's political police apparatus as it exists today was born. This article explains the political battles within the workers movement over how to combat government and employer attacks against the working class and unions, the Black rights movement, Puerto Rican independence fighters, opponents of US wars, and others. In *New International no. 6*. $16. Also in Spanish.

Problems of Women's Liberation
EVELYN REED

Six articles explore the social and economic roots of women's oppression from prehistoric society to modern capitalism and point the road forward to emancipation. $15

www.pathfinderpress.com

Malcolm X Talks to Young People

"You're living at a time of revolution," Malcolm told young people in the United Kingdom in December 1964. "And I for one will join in with anyone, I don't care what color you are, as long as you want to change the miserable condition that exists on this earth." Four talks and an interview given to young people in Ghana, the UK, and the United States in the last months of Malcolm's life. $15. Also in Spanish.

Capitalism and the Transformation of Africa
Reports from Equatorial Guinea
MARY-ALICE WATERS, MARTÍN KOPPEL

An account of the transformation of class relations in this Central African country, as it is drawn deeper into the world market and both a capitalist class and modern proletariat are born. The example of Cuba's socialist revolution comes alive in the collaboration of Cuban volunteer medical brigades there. Woven together, the outlines of a future to be fought for today can be seen—a future in which Africa's toilers have more weight in world politics than ever before. $10. Also in Spanish.

The Jewish Question
A Marxist Interpretation
ABRAM LEON

Traces the historical rationalizations of anti-Semitism to the fact that, in the centuries preceding the domination of industrial capitalism, Jews emerged as a "people-class" of merchants, moneylenders, and traders. Leon explains why the propertied rulers incite renewed Jew-hatred in the epoch of capitalism's decline. $22

www.pathfinderpress.com

Is Socialist Revolution in the U.S. Possible?
A Necessary Debate
MARY-ALICE WATERS

"To think a socialist revolution in the US is not possible, you'd have to believe not only that the wealthy ruling families and their economic wizards have found a way to 'manage' capitalism. You'd have to close your eyes to the spreading imperialist wars and economic, financial, and social crises we are in the midst of." —Mary-Alice Waters.

In talks given as part of a wide-ranging debate at the 2007 and 2008 Venezuela Book Fairs, Waters explains why a socialist revolution is not only possible, but why revolutionary struggles by working people are inevitable—battles forced on us by the rulers' crisis-driven assaults on our living and job conditions, on our very humanity. $7. Also in Spanish, French, and Swedish.

Cuba and the Coming American Revolution
JACK BARNES

The Cuban Revolution of 1959 had a worldwide political impact, including on working people and youth in the US. In the early 1960s, says Barnes, "the mass proletarian-based struggle to bring down Jim Crow segregation in the South was marching toward bloody victories as the Cuban Revolution was advancing." The deep-going social transformation Cuban toilers fought for and won set an example that socialist revolution is not only necessary—it can be made and defended by workers and farmers in the imperialist heartland as well. Foreword by Mary-Alice Waters. $10. Also in Spanish and French.

www.pathfinderpress.com

Teamster Rebellion
FARRELL DOBBS

The first of a four-volume participant's account of how strikes and organizing drives across the Midwest in the 1930s, initiated by leaders of Teamsters Local 574 in Minneapolis, paved the way for industrial unions and a fighting working-class social movement. These battles showed what workers and farmers can achieve when they have the leadership they deserve. Dobbs was a central part of that class-struggle leadership. $19. Also in Spanish, French, and Swedish.

Fighting Racism in World War II
From the Pages of the Militant

An account from 1939 to 1945 of struggles against racism and lynch-mob terror in face of patriotic appeals to postpone resistance until after US "victory" in World War II. These struggles—of a piece with anti-imperialist battles the world over—helped lay the basis for the mass Black rights movement in the 1950s and '60s. $25

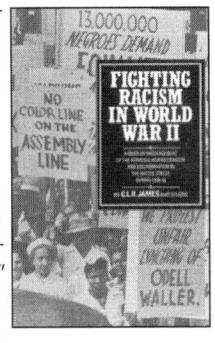

The First Ten Years of American Communism
JAMES P. CANNON

A founding leader of the communist movement in the US recounts early efforts to build a proletarian party emulating the Bolshevik leadership of the October 1917 revolution in Russia. $22

Revolutionary Continuity
Marxist Leadership in the U.S.
FARRELL DOBBS

How successive generations of fighters joined in struggles that shaped the US labor movement, seeking to build a revolutionary leadership able to advance the interests of workers and small farmers and link up with fellow toilers worldwide. 2 vols. *The Early Years: 1848–1917,* $20; *Birth of the Communist Movement: 1918–1922,* $19.

From the dictatorship of capital...

The Communist Manifesto
Karl Marx, Frederick Engels

Founding document of the modern revolutionary workers movement, published in 1848. Why communism is not a set of preconceived principles but the line of march of the working class toward power—a line of march "springing from an existing class struggle, a historical movement going on under our very eyes." $5. Also in Spanish, French, and Arabic.

State and Revolution
V.I. Lenin

"The relation of the socialist proletarian revolution to the state is acquiring not only practical political importance," wrote V.I. Lenin in this booklet just months before the October 1917 Russian Revolution. It also addresses the "most urgent problem of the day: explaining to the masses what they will have to do to free themselves from capitalist tyranny." In *Essential Works of Lenin*. $12.95

Their Trotsky and Ours
Jack Barnes

To lead the working class in a successful revolution, a mass proletarian party is needed whose cadres, well beforehand, have absorbed a world communist program, are proletarian in life and work, derive deep satisfaction from doing politics, and have forged a leadership with an acute sense of what to do next. This book is about building such a party. $16. Also in Spanish and French.

www.pathfinderpress.com

...to the dictatorship of the proletariat

Lenin's Final Fight
Speeches and Writings, 1922–23
V.I. Lenin

In 1922 and 1923, V.I. Lenin, central leader of the world's first socialist revolution, waged what was to be his last political battle. At stake was whether that revolution would remain on the proletarian course that had brought workers and peasants to power in October 1917—and laid the foundations for a truly worldwide revolutionary movement of toilers organizing to emulate the Bolsheviks' example. $20. Also in Spanish.

Trade Unions: Their Past, Present, and Future
Karl Marx

Apart from being instruments "required for guerrilla fights between capital and labor," the unions "must now act deliberately as organizing centers of the working class in the broad interest of its complete emancipation," through revolutionary political action. Drafted by Marx for the First International's founding congress in 1866, this resolution appears in *Trade Unions in the Epoch of Imperialist Decay* by Leon Trotsky. $16

The History of the Russian Revolution
Leon Trotsky

The social, economic, and political dynamics of the first socialist revolution as told by one of its central leaders. How, under Lenin's leadership, the Bolshevik Party led the overturn of the monarchist regime of the landlords and capitalists and brought to power a government of the workers and peasants. Unabridged, 3 vols. in one. $38. Also in Russian.

New International

A MAGAZINE OF MARXIST POLITICS AND THEORY

NEW INTERNATIONAL NO. 12

CAPITALISM'S LONG HOT WINTER HAS BEGUN

Jack Barnes

and *"Their Transformation and Ours,"* Resolution of the Socialist Workers Party

Today's sharpening interimperialist conflicts are fueled both by the opening stages of what will be decades of economic, financial, and social convulsions and class battles, and by the most far-reaching shift in Washington's military policy and organization since the US buildup toward World War II. Class-struggle-minded working people must face this historic turning point for imperialism, and draw satisfaction from being "in their face" as we chart a revolutionary course to confront it. $16

NEW INTERNATIONAL NO. 13

OUR POLITICS START WITH THE WORLD

Jack Barnes

The huge economic and cultural inequalities between imperialist and semicolonial countries, and among classes within almost every country, are produced, reproduced, and accentuated by the workings of capitalism. For vanguard workers to build parties able to lead a successful revolutionary struggle for power in our own countries, says Jack Barnes in the lead article, our activity must be guided by a strategy to close this gap.

Also in No. 13: "Farming, Science, and the Working Classes" *by Steve Clark.* $14

THESE ISSUES ARE ALSO AVAILABLE IN SPANISH, FRENCH, AND SWEDISH AT
WWW.PATHFINDERPRESS.COM